LIFE OF THE TRAIL 3 THE HISTORIC ROUTE

FROM OLD BOW FORT TO JASPER

LIFE OF THE TRAIL 3 THE HISTORIC ROUTE
FROM OLD BOW FORT TO JASPER

By Emerson Sanford & Janice Sanford Beck

Rocky Mountain Books
VANCOUVER • VICTORIA • CALGARY

Rocky Mountain Books	Rocky Mountain Books
#108 – 17665 66A Avenue	PO Box 468
Surrey, BC V3S 2A7	Custer, WA
www.rmbooks.com	98240-0468

Library and Archives Canada Cataloguing in Publication

Sanford, Emerson
The historic route from Old Bow Fort to Jasper / Emerson Sanford & Janice Sanford Beck.

(Life of the trail 3)
Includes bibliographical references and index.

ISBN 978-1-897522-41-7

1. Hiking—Rocky Mountains, Canadian (B.C. and Alta.)—Guidebooks.
2. Trails—Rocky Mountains, Canadian (B.C. and Alta.)—Guidebooks.
3. Hiking—Rocky Mountains, Canadian (B.C. and Alta.)—History.
4. Rocky Mountains, Canadian (B.C. and Alta.)—Guidebooks.
5. Mountaineers—Rocky Mountains, Canadian (B.C. and Alta.)—Biography. I. Sanford Beck, Janice, 1975- II. Title. III. Series.

GV199.44.C22A45843 2009   796.51097123'32   C2008-907156-5

Front cover photo by Emerson Sanford
Back cover photo courtesy of The Whyte Museum of the Canadian Rockies Archives (V653/NG-4-278)
All interior images supplied by the authors unless otherwise noted.

Printed in Canada

Rocky Mountain Books acknowledges the financial support for its publishing program from the Government of Canada through the Book Publishing Industry Development Program (BPIDP), Canada Council for the Arts and the province of British Columbia through the British Columbia Arts Council and the Book Publishing Tax Credit.

Disclaimer

The actions described in this book may be considered inherently dangerous activities. Individuals undertake these activities at their own risk. The information put forth in this guide has been collected from a variety of sources and is not guaranteed to be completely accurate or reliable. Many conditions and some information may change owing to weather and numerous other factors beyond the control of the authors and publishers. Individual climbers and/or hikers must determine the risks, use their own judgment and take full responsibility for their actions. Do not depend on any information found in this book for your own personal safety. Your safety depends on your own good judgment based on your skills, education and experience.

It is up to the users of this guidebook to acquire the necessary skills for safe experiences and to exercise caution in potentially hazardous areas. The authors and publishers of this guide accept no responsibility for your actions or the results that occur from another's actions, choices or judgments. If you have any doubt as to your safety or your ability to attempt anything described in this guidebook, do not attempt it.

It seems a bit sad to me that the road is going up into the country where we had so much fun. It was about the last stand of the pack-train, and it is a shame to trade that experience for the sake of the few cars that will rush through. Someday when you [Jimmy Simpson] are running a garage and tea-room at Bow Lake, and want to see how cayuses look, just run down here and I'll show you some movies of the good old days.

—J. Monroe Thorington[1]

Contents

Acknowledgements

The preparation for a book of this type requires the perusal of many secondary sources; during our research we read hundreds of books. The authors of these works are acknowledged in the Notes section at the end of this book. Many of the books are still in print and readily available. Others required much diligence on the part of reference librarians to obtain using interlibrary loans, and we wish to thank the personnel at the Canmore Public Library, especially Michelle Preston and Hélène Lafontaine, for their assistance. Other books and documents were available only through the Whyte Museum and Archives, and we appreciate the efforts of Lena Goon, Elizabeth Kundert-Cameron, D.L. Cameron and Ted Hart for steering us on the right track and obtaining materials for us.

The Alpine Club of Canada in Canmore kindly allowed us the use of their collection of the *Canadian Alpine Journal.* Chief Ernest Wesley of the Stoney First Nations willingly permitted us to explore and photograph the site of Old Bow Fort. Others who provided useful discussion and/or materials during the course of the research were: Carol at the Bruce Peel Special Collections Library at the University of Alberta, who was diligent in her search for the J.N. Wallace Manuscript Collection; Lorna Dishkin of the BC Central Coast Archives; Keith Cole; Rene Morton; Mary and Bob Smith; Thomas Peterson; and I.S. MacLaren.

A large part of the effort in preparing these volumes was in hiking all of the trails and routes described in the history section. Emerson wishes to thank his wife, Cheryl, for the many hours that she spent taking him to trailheads and picking him up several days later at a different location, sometimes on remote gravel roads that were not easily accessible. Several trips along the highway from Canmore to Jasper and on to Mount Robson were required to complete all of the hikes in the series.

For Janice, this project has been a labour of love, squeezed in amongst various family, community and work responsibilities. She would like to thank her partner, Shawn, and children, Rowan, Christopher and Robin, for their willingness to accommodate the time required for a project of this magnitude. She would also like to thank her parents for sharing their love of history and introducing her to the trails these volumes bring to life.

Finally, the authors would like to express their appreciation to Don Gorman, Meaghan Craven, Chyla Cardinal and others at Rocky Mountain Books for their efforts in bringing this work from manuscript to publication.

Ruffed grouse were often seen along the trail in the early days of pack trains, and they often ended up in the stewpot. Outfitters frequently carried pistols, which they used to harvest the birds. The grouse seemed not to fear humans, which allowed the men to shoot them at close range.

Introduction

Like mountaineer and explorer J. Monroe Thorington, many of the early tourist-explorers in the Canadian Rockies lamented the development of roads through their beloved wilderness. Perhaps more than any other area covered in this series, the Bow Valley and Icefields Parkway corridor has been drastically transformed by the desire of the federal government to improve its accessibility to the travelling public. The process of this transformation can be tracked through four distinct periods of exploration, ranging from pre-contact Aboriginal travels through to post-railway pleasure travellers.

The Aboriginal peoples of western North America have been negotiating the valleys and passes of this region for millennia. Archaeological evidence indicates that 11,000 years ago, Aboriginal peoples feasted on mountain sheep while camped along the Bow River. Abundant game was not the only reason First Peoples entered the mountains; the Aboriginal peoples of the plains and the interior mountains traded extensively, and many of their travels through the Rockies appear to have been for trading purposes. There is evidence, for example, that bands of Shuswap travelling from interior British Columbia camped at the junction of the Bow and Spray rivers three thousand years ago. It was these early travellers who established the north–south route along the Bow River that today's alpine travellers know so well. But because Aboriginal travels through the Rockies were generally not recorded, very little is known of this first period of exploration.

The second phase of Rocky Mountain exploration began in the early nineteenth century, as European fur traders began to seek passage to the West Coast. Most were guided by Aboriginal or Métis men whose ancestors had been travelling the trails for centuries, but the fur traders' single-minded focus on finding navigable routes across the mountains limited the extent of their exploration. They travelled no farther north than necessary to finding a westward passage.

Once fur traders had broached the mountains, however, it was only a matter of time before other easterners followed suit. Scientists and railway men undertook the third period of exploration between the 1858 Palliser Expedition to Western Canada and the 1885 completion of the Canadian Pacific Railway. As the fur trade began to subside, the British – and later Canadian – governments grew keen to secure their claim to the West. They sent surveyors and scientists to collect as much information as possible, hoping they might be able to promote settlement in the area. The Palliser Expedition's James Hector travelled widely through the region, exploring the passes for possible transportation corridors and collecting data on the region's geology, flora and fauna. Later explorations resumed focus on finding a route through the mountains – this time for the railway.

As soon as trains could pass successfully through the Rockies, there was no restraining the pleasure travellers of the fourth period of exploration. Whether motivated by the thrill of discovery, the desire to scale unknown peaks, a passion for the hunt or simply the desire to bask in the solitude of the wilderness, these intrepid individuals undertook a variety of journeys, following routes that have become today's mountain highways.

In their day, of course, there were no vehicles whizzing along alpine roads; everything they needed for their lengthy explorations had to be carried by pack train – most led by professional guides and outfitters. The guides' efforts to safely lead their clients through mountainous and sometimes dangerous terrain substantially increased the number of identifiable trails through the Rockies.

In 1885 the Banff Hot Springs Reserve was set aside as a national preserve and expanded into Rocky Mountains Park (today's Banff National Park) two years later. The less accessible region that constitutes today's Jasper National Park was first protected by the federal government in 1907. With the 1909 institution of the Fire and Game Guardians in Rocky Mountains Park, trails took another giant step toward becoming the readily identifiable routes we know today.

Park officials decided that instituting a network of trails would substantially simplify the guardians' work in enforcing park regulations. By 1914 the guardian service reported some 60 trails through the park, all of which were being regularly patrolled. By 1920 the Fire and Game Guardian Service had become the Warden Service and was patrolling 1,400 miles (2253 kilometres) of trails through the park. Wardens curious about the surrounding areas often explored side valleys along their patrols, thus establishing at least some of the non-historic trails within the parks.

By the mid-1930s, technological innovations in camping supplies had begun to transform the nature of alpine travel. Steel-framed backpacks, lightweight tents and sleeping bags, and Primus stoves all meant that individuals could spend two weeks on the trail without need for pack trains or guides. The era of the pack train was over. Since then, very few new trails have been established in the Rockies; of the few that have been cut, most have realigned or replaced existing trails for environmental reasons.

By the 1920s, automobile use had also begun to significantly increase the number of visitors to Canada's Rocky Mountain parks. By 1921 a motor road had been built as far as Lake Louise. Ten years later, construction began on the Banff–Jasper Highway; its 1940 opening dramatically transformed the nature of travel through the Rockies. For the first time, large numbers of people were travelling through the region in a north–south direction.

The dominant presence of the road from Old Bow Fort to Jasper has also affected the format of this book. *The Life of the Trail* series divides historic routes through the Rockies into regions based primarily on geographical boundaries that influenced nineteenth-century travellers. The series presents volumes in order of entry by non-Aboriginal explorers, and routes within each volume are described in order of first use. Each book, designed to fit neatly into a pack, outlines the history of the routes in its region, giving modern-day travellers a feel for how they were established and who has used the trails since.

Life of the Trail 1 records historic routes and hikes in the area bounded by the North Saskatchewan River on the north and the Mistaya River, Bow River and Lake Minnewanka on the west and south. The most historically significant trip in this area was David Thompson's journey along the Red Deer River to meet the Kootenay people and take them back to Rocky Mountain House. Later, the Aboriginal route over Pipestone Pass to the Kootenay Plains was used extensively by tourist-explorers and mountaineers. Today this area is bounded by the David Thompson Highway (#11) in the north and the Icefields Parkway (#93), the Bow Valley Parkway (#1A) and Lake Minnewanka on the west and south.

The earliest fur-trade route across the Rockies was over Howse Pass. The trail is described in *Life of the Trail 2*, which presents the area bounded by the Kicking Horse River to the south; the Columbia Icefield to the north; and the Bow, Mistaya and North Saskatchewan rivers to the east. Later explorers created a popular return trip from the Kootenay Plains by adding an old Native trail down the Amiskwi River to the Howse Pass route. Also included in the volume are the Yoho Valley and the Castleguard Meadows. Today that area is bounded by the Trans-Canada Highway to the south and the Icefields Parkway to the east.

This third volume in the series describes a single route. It follows the Bow River to Bow Pass, and then the Mistaya, North Saskatchewan, Sunwapta and Athabasca rivers to the junction with the Miette. Today this is the route of the Trans-Canada Highway and Highway 1A to Lake

Louise and the Icefields Parkway north to Jasper. For the sake of clarity, the route has been divided into three sections, presented in the order of first use by non-Aboriginal travellers.

Each section begins with a brief overview of the history of that portion of the trail, followed by stories of the known travellers who helped make it what it is today. When we use the first person "I" in the introductory material, the "I" is Emerson sharing stories of his own adventures along the route. But where other volumes continue with a complete trail guide for the modern traveller, this volume only describes one trail that can be easily hiked: it is drivers, rather than hikers, who will be best able to follow the rest of the route.

With a little imagination, today's park visitors and armchair travellers alike can imagine British Army Lieutenants Henry J. Warre and Mervin Vavasour travelling west over White Man Pass on a trail that, mere weeks later, Father Pierre Jean de Smet would use to enter the Bow Valley. You can share in the excitement as CPR men scout out a route for the cross-country railway. You can hold your breath as climbers J. Norman Collie, Hugh Stutfield and Herman Woolley catch the first glimpse of the Columbia Icefield; join Mary Schäffer and Mollie Adams in becoming the first non-Aboriginal women to view much of the area that constitutes today's Banff and Jasper national parks; and watch Byron Harmon film his 70-day pack trip from Banff to Jasper.

But the imagination requires more strength here than in other parts of the Rockies. Change in this area has been so significant that not even the most adventurous can properly follow in the footsteps of these early adventurers. The lament in Jimmy Simpson's response to Thorington is not misplaced:

> I feel like you as regards the motor road up into the north country. When I recall the old days when I used to snowshoe and sleep out at night under the stars & a spruce with 20 below as the only covering it makes me feel that I don't want to see the same landmarks from an auto. I suppose the wind will blow with the same frigidity: the same ridges

will be windswept and the same hollows will be drifted full even though the motor road passes over or by them, but to me the landscape will hold a blight or a scar that will never heal.[2]

Mule deer, like this young buck in early summer velvet, can be seen all along the route between Old Bow Fort and Lake Louise.

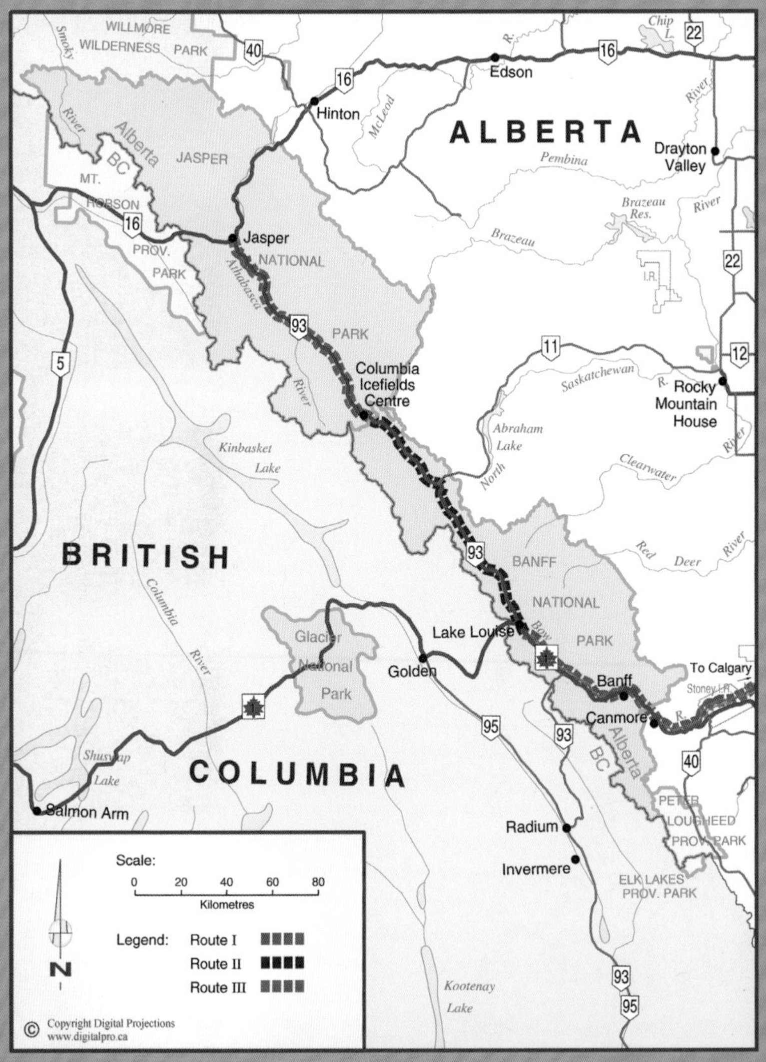

The historic trail from Old Bow Fort (Morley) to Fitzhugh (Jasper).

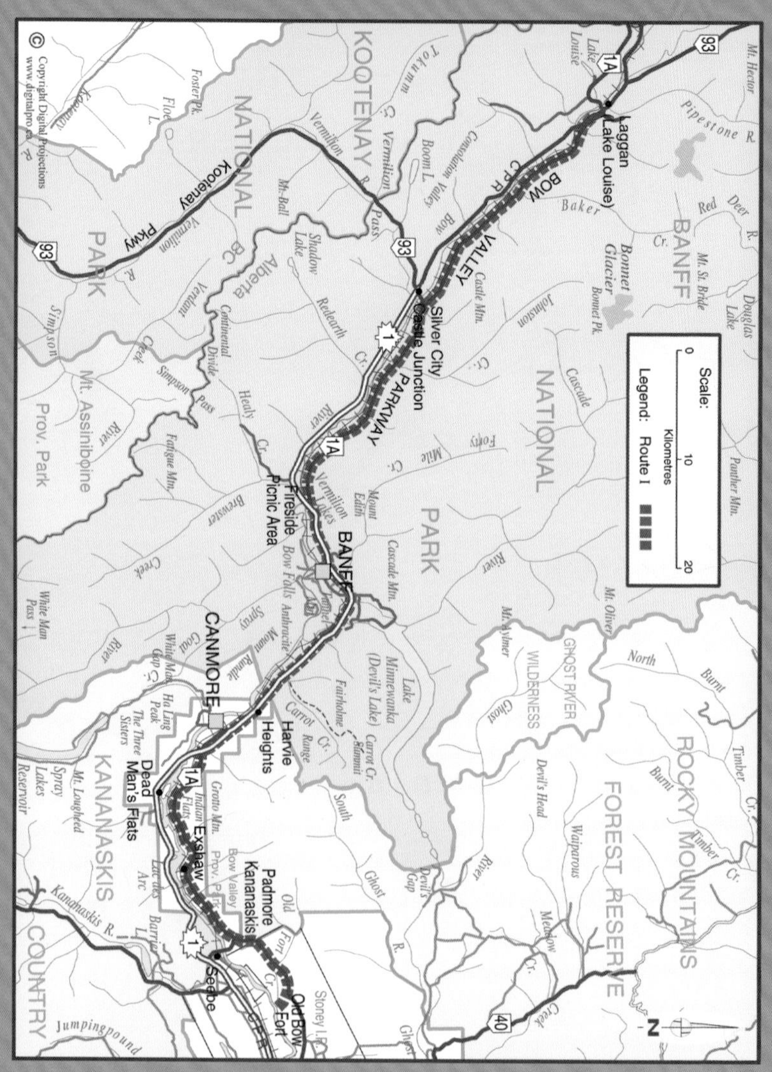

The historic trail from Old Bow Fort (Morley) to Laggan (Lake Louise).

Route I

Route of the Railway: Old Bow Fort to Laggan (Lake Louise)

In the nineteenth century, any European travelling along the Bow River would have stopped at the remains of the Hudson's Bay Company's (HBC) Peigan Post, or Old Bow Fort. Though it was destroyed less than a year after its completion, reports indicated that its remains are still visible, and I was anxious to see them. In late June 2004, my wife, Cheryl, and I left Canmore for the Morley Reserve. We hoped to obtain the Stoneys' permission to visit and photograph the site and to receive directions to its exact location.

Travelling east on Highway 1A, we passed the Seebe exit (Highway 1X) and continued on a short distance until we reached a small creek. According to our map, this should have been Old Fort Creek. But with the highway some distance north of the Bow River at that point, we could not discern the river's exact location. We continued driving until we came to a road leading off to the right, which appeared to reach to the river somewhere near the mouth of the creek.

Though we had intended to obtain permission to visit the site from someone in Morley, we could not resist the call of this gravel road. On we went, mainly hoping to determine if this was indeed the location of

Old Bow Fort. We soon reached a group of locals preparing for a major gathering at a picnic site. I approached the nearest person, described my mission and asked from whom I should seek permission. The man simply pointed to the person next to him, with whom he had been talking. That person soon started asking me questions: who was I, who did I work for and exactly why did I want to visit the site? Satisfied about my intentions, he introduced himself as Ernest Wesley, the chief of the local band and indicated that we were welcome to explore and photograph the site as much as we desired.

Considering ourselves extremely lucky to have happened upon the chief, we continued the short distance to the site – now quite visible from the road – and spent the next few hours walking about. Standing high above the Bow River, it was easy to imagine James Hector and his party preparing to enter the mountains, the Earl of Southesk and his men happy to be leaving the mountains, and the Overlanders headed for the goldfields of British Columbia, gathering strength for the next stage of their journey, full of trepidation about what lay ahead.

Peigan Post was built on the Bow River in 1832. This is an artist's conception of what the fort would have looked like. The fort was abandoned in 1834 and subsequently burned. The remains of Peigan Post became known as Old Bow Fort.

Chronology

9000 BC Aboriginal Peoples camp along the Bow River and feast on mountain sheep.

1000 BC Shuswap bands from the interior mountains camp at the junction of the Bow and Spray rivers.

1787 David Thompson views the Rocky Mountains from the foothills.

1800 Duncan McGillivray and David Thompson follow the Bow River west into the mountains.

1832 Peigan Post is built at the junction of the Bow River and Old Fort Creek.

1834 Peigan Post is abandoned by the fur traders and destroyed by the Natives. The ruins of Peigan Post become known as Old Bow Fort.

1841 Sir George Simpson enters the mountains through Devil's Gap then proceeds to the Bow Valley.

James Sinclair leads a party of 116 Red River Métis through Devil's Gap to Lake Minnewanka and over Carrot Creek Summit to the Bow Valley. He leaves the valley via White Man Gap.

1844 Reverend Robert Rundle enters the mountains from Old Bow Fort and attempts to climb a nearby mountain.

1845 In July, British Army Lieutenants Henry J. Warre and Mervin Vavasour, led by Peter Skene Ogden, follow the Bow River from Old Bow Fort to Canmore, where they cross the Bow and head south over White Man Pass.

A few weeks later, Father Pierre Jean de Smet crosses White Man Pass in the opposite direction and enters the Bow Valley. He spends little time there before leaving via Old Bow Fort.

1847 Reverend Robert Rundle again enters the mountains via Old Bow Fort and goes west along the Bow to Lake Minnewanka. He leaves the mountains through Devil's Gap.

1854 James Sinclair is back at Old Bow Fort with one hundred more Métis immigrants. They turn south along the Kananaskis River and cross North Kananaskis Pass.

1858 Captain John Palliser and James Hector of the Palliser Expedition enter the mountains along the Bow River and proceed to Old Bow Fort. From there, Palliser follows Sinclair's route south along the Kananaskis River, and Hector proceeds west along the Bow as far as Castle Mountain, where he turns south.

1859 Hector returns to the Bow Valley on August 23, this time following the Bow as far as Laggan, where he turns north along the Pipestone River.

Ten days later, the Earl of Southesk and his party travel south along the same route. Southesk follows the Bow to Old Bow Fort and out of the mountains.

Several groups of Overlanders meet at Old Bow Fort at different times in the fall then follow Sinclair and Palliser's route over North Kananaskis Pass, heading for central British Columbia's Fraser River goldfields.

1861 The Reid party of Overlanders passes through Old Bow Fort on its way along the Bow River to Vermilion Pass and the Columbia River.

1879 John Macoun, survey naturalist with the Geological Survey of Canada, visits the Bow Valley, travelling from Old Bow Fort to Cascade Mountain.

1880s Major Rogers and his assistant, Tom Wilson, herd pack horses up the Bow Valley, clearing and widening the old Native trail as they go.

1881 The Canadian Pacific Railway (CPR) scouts and surveyors reach Exshaw.

1883 Sandford Fleming, who was in charge of the overall CPR survey, travels along the Bow River and then west to the top of Kicking Horse Pass.

1884 After a winter of heavy snow and a warm spring, the snow melts so quickly that the Bow River channel can not contain the deluge. The overflow causes major property damage.

Siding 27 in the Bow Valley is completed and renamed Canmore, after King Malcolm of Canmore, Scotland. Coal is discovered in Canmore that same year. Within three years, Canmore has become a thriving coal-mining town.

A boom town called Silver City develops near the base of Castle Mountain.

Explorer and mountaineer Professor A.P. Coleman stops in Silver City.

1885 Hopes of a significant ore strike diminish and Silver City becomes a ghost town almost overnight.

The railway is completed along the Bow and west to the Kicking Horse valley.

The first transcontinental passenger train chugs along what was the old Native trail.

Banff Hot Springs Reserve is set aside as a protected area.

1887 Banff Hot Springs Reserve is expanded and becomes Rocky Mountains Park.

The booming community of Kananaskis is already home to at least 30 people and boasts a sawmill, limestone quarry, railway station, water tower and section house.

1888 The railway moves the station from Siding 29, near the base of Cascade Mountain, to the present site of the Town of Banff. The people living at the old station site soon move to the new town. By 1897 Siding 29 is gone.

William Spotswood Green, an English minister, visits Joe Smith, the only resident of Silver City.

1890 The Reverend Charles W. Gordon arrives in Canmore to take charge of Presbyterian parishes in Banff, Canmore and Anthracite, as well as any lumber camps in the area.

1891 John Macoun returns to the Bow Valley in order to make a representative collection of the flora and fauna of Rocky Mountains Park.

1893 Two Morley Natives, William and Joshua Twin, and their families trail a small herd of horses from Morley to Laggan along the railway tote road in order to transport a group of American tourists from the village to the lake.

1897 John Macoun returns to the Bow Valley to complete his collection.

1902 The Bow River floods again, causing the railway to shut down for six days. Roadways along the river require major repairs.

1907 The town of Exshaw, just west of the old settlement of Kananaskis, boasts about 20 buildings as a result of a new cement plant.

1909 The Calgary–Banff Coach Road is completed.

1915 A good gravel road is completed to Castle Junction, at which point two hundred detainees from the Lethbridge internment camp transfer to Castle Mountain and work on the section to Lake Louise. They labour on the road during the summers of 1915 and 1916.

1916 Dr. Charles Walcott travels along the Bow River by buckboard from Old Bow Fort to Lake Louise. He makes similar trips in 1917, 1919 and 1921.

1921 The gravel road is completed from Castle Junction to Lake Louise.

1933 Cliff and Ruth Kopas trail their five horses along the road to Lake Louise, part of an overland trip to Bella Coola (on the Pacific Coast).

History

First Peoples

Aboriginal peoples have been travelling the Bow River corridor for thousands of years. A 1969 archaeological study identified 48 sites along the river.[1] Additional studies along the Vermilion Lakes (close to the Bow River near present-day Banff) in the 1980s indicate that early visitors camped and feasted on mountain sheep in the area 11,000 years ago. Campsites identified on the riverside terrace near the foot of Mount Edith have been dated at more than 9,500 years old. And the alluvial plain between the Bow and Spray rivers revealed remains of distinctive pit houses used on a regular basis by the Shuswap people from the interior mountains approximately 3,000 years ago.[2]

Aboriginal activity in the area is almost certainly linked to the naming of the Bow River, but it has been difficult to pinpoint exactly how. In 1961 historian James Wallace, who has written extensively on the fur trade and

The Vermilion Lakes, just west of Banff, were first visited about 11,000 years ago and have been a favourite stopping place ever since. Nestled between the railroad and the Trans-Canada Highway, the lakes provide a scenic foreground for views of Mount Rundle and surrounding peaks.

mountain history, claimed that "[i]t is from the Douglas Fir that the Bow takes its name, for in the early days the wood of this tree was used by the Indian of the plains for making bows, long before the advent of the white man."[3]

It is true that isolated pockets of Douglas fir grow along the Bow River near present-day Canmore and likely in other spots in the Bow Valley. These trees have a thick bark and can withstand most forest fires. As a result, there would have been a continual supply of these slow-growing trees. However, the wood's attributes make the suggestion that local peoples used the limbs to make bows extremely unlikely.

The name more likely derives from the bow reed, a species of yew, similar to Saskatoon bushes. In *Canmore and Kananaskis Country*, Gillean Daffern explains that "the Stonies call the Bow River *Mini thni Wapta* 'cold river' or *Ijathibe Wapta*, 'bow river', or *Manachaban*, 'the river where the bow reed grows'. This refers to Saskatoon saplings used to make bows for hunting."[4]

David Thompson's journals from his first visit to the southern Alberta foothills in 1787 support Daffern's theory. Thompson recorded that the river derived its name from a species of yew that grew on its banks. This tree was first described by botanist David Douglas in 1826 and has been named *Pseudotsuga douglasii*, which can be freely translated as "like a yew, but not really a yew."[5] Thompson himself is probably responsible for shortening the name from "the river where the bow reed grows" to simply the Bow River.[6]

These bow reeds played a significant role in the local economy. The four-foot (1.2-metre) bows fashioned from them both met the needs that could be supplied by a successful hunt and also became a valuable trade item. Banff historian Eleanor Luxton reported that "[t]he bows were curved on either side of the hand grip and points, and were bound with sinew. So desirable were these bows that even a horse would be traded for one."[7]

Douglas fir trees, such as these growing east of Canmore, have a very thick bark that enables them to withstand the ravages of forest fires. Although they would have been available to Aboriginal bow makers, conifer limbs are known to bend without breaking and to hold that shape without springing back, the opposite property to that required for making bows.

THE FUR TRADE

The trails that Aboriginal peoples used to gather yew, track their game and connect with trade partners were likely instrumental in guiding the first white men to enter the mountains along the Bow. Fur traders Duncan McGillivray and David Thompson were undoubtedly following an old Native trail when they headed west along the river late in the fall of 1800.

Thompson had the distinction of being one of the first white men to view the mountains. Having spent the winter of 1787–88 with a Peigan band in the foothills, he would have seen the mountains from somewhere near the beginning of the Bow River's journey through the prairies.[8] He wrote in his diary: "[t]he Rocky Mountains came in sight like shining white clouds on the horizon. As we proceeded they rose in height; their immense masses of snow appeared above the clouds forming an impassable barrier, even to an eagle."[9] Beholding that view was as close as he came to the mountains that year.

In 1800 the North West Company posted David Thompson to the fort at Rocky Mountain House. The company was anxious to establish trade with the Aboriginal peoples west of the mountains. Duncan McGillivray, Thompson's superior, was responsible for finding a route. McGillivray arrived at the fort shortly after Thompson. In November McGillivray, Thompson and four French Canadian voyageurs set out on an exploratory trip along the foothills. Their dual objectives were to visit a Peigan band on the Highwood River in the southern end of the Kananaskis valley and search out passes through the mountains.[10]

Returning from their November 1800 visit with the Peigans, Thompson and McGillivray forded the Bow River (probably somewhere near today's Morley Bridge) and followed it west along what would later become the route of Highway 1A. On December 1, they terminated their westward travels and climbed a mountain to view the lay of the land. The peak was likely Loder Peak, near present-day Exshaw, just west of where Old Bow Fort was eventually located. They returned to their horses four hours later, thus ending the first recorded ascent in the Canadian Rockies. After crossing the Bow and Ghost rivers, the men retraced their route through the foothills to the fort at Rocky Mountain House.

By 1830 the North West Company had merged with the Hudson's Bay Company under the latter name, and the newly expanded company was very interested in following up on the North West Company's initial foray into Blackfoot country in order to establish trade with the Peigans. Their strategy: to build a fort on the Bow River to better access Peigan furs.

Opposite: David Thompson, geographer, surveyor and map maker, took celestial observations wherever he went. He later used the data collected to draw remarkably accurate maps of the North-West.

Right: The Bow River just west of the Morley Bridge. The river's width at this point indicates that it is quite shallow, ideal for a ford. The river today is likely wider than it was two hundred years ago, due to the hydroelectric dam downstream.

Old Bow Fort

The remains of Old Bow Fort are located on the Morley Reserve on a high plateau overlooking the junction of Old Fort Creek and the Bow River. Although the fort was evidently built during the fur-trade era, historians spent years puzzling over its name. There was no reference to "Old Bow Fort" in HBC literature. The only clue researchers could find was documentation of the 1832 decision to close the post at Rocky Mountain House in order to build Peigan Post on the Bow River and – it was hoped – attract trade with the Peigans.[11]

That summer, Chief Factor John Rowand and Henry Fisher, the clerk who had been in charge of Rocky Mountain House, travelled up the Bow River to select a site. Fisher was left to supervise his crew of ten men in the construction of the new post. John Harriott, who was to be responsible for the post, arrived on October 10 with a clerk and 16 men. Construction continued through the winter, but as the post was only to be used during the winter, it was vacated in the spring. Over the summer, local peoples damaged the new post. It was reopened on August 10, but the hopes with which Peigan Post had been built were not realized. The decision

Right: This sketch of Old Bow Fort indicates the locations of the 11 chimneys that were visible to historian J.N. Wallace in 1924.

Opposite: Peigan Post was built on a plateau high above the mouth of Old Fort Creek at the Bow River. The ravine, to the right of the creek and the river, may have been the source of some of the logs used to build the fort.

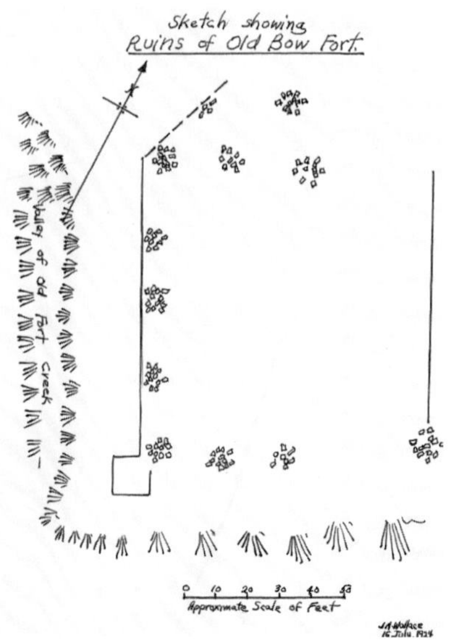

was made to abandon the post and reopen Rocky Mountain House. On January 8, 1834, Peigan Post was left "to the mercy of the Sarcees who lost no time in taking possession."[12]

Historian J.N. Wallace was the first to make the link between this post and the Old Bow Fort referred to by later travellers:

> My own view is that this is one of those cases where a name has persisted in a manner quite unjustified by its own importance.... This fictitious fame of a place of secondary importance may be explained by its being the only place in a large area which had a name, so that people came to use it to localise their travels and other events.... [T]he present ruins known as 'Old Bow Fort'... may be Peigan Post established by the H. B. Co. in year 1832.... The old name 'Old Bow Fort' would naturally be used instead of the official name 'Peigan Post', and the latter would be forgotten.[13]

It seems that while the record-keepers at York Factory focused on trade with the Peigans and referred to Peigan Post, those who came later used geographical indicators to refer to the fort.[14] From a practical perspective, Old Bow Fort now refers to the ruins of Peigan Post. Because of its location on the Bow River, because the remains of the old fort remained visible for more than a century and because it was the only location in southern Alberta that had an English name at that time, it is natural that virtually all early eastern travellers who entered the mountains along the Bow would refer to "Old Bow Fort."

Old Bow Fort (photographed in June 2004) is still visible today as piles of stones that were probably fireplaces 175 years ago.

Despite the fact that the fort – or Peigan Post – was occupied for only five months, its considerable size indicates that it was intended as a post of some importance. Based on what remained in 1931, historian J.E.A. Macleod concluded:

> It was apparently a five-sided stockaded post, the rear or western wall being roughly parallel with the edge of the ravine at the bottom of which flows the creek. The entrance was in the front or eastern wall, while the north end of the post was in the form of an acute angle. The buildings evidently were ranged along the south and western walls, and in a line forming the base of the triangle of which the two northern walls were the sides, and all faced upon a central court or quadrangle. The ruins of one fireplace are somewhat isolated from the others, and the building of which it formed a part would appear either to have been outside the stockade or to have formed the south-eastern corner of it. In either case it probably was the Indian Hall, which in fur-trading posts was usually situated so as to admit Indians to trade without giving them access to the post. At the south-west corner of the post there are plain traces of a block-house bastion from which the occupants of the fort could command with their fire the southern and western walls. There are no discernible traces of any other bastion; probably the Indian Hall, if built in the stockade, would serve the same purpose for the front wall.[15]

When Palliser visited in 1858, the 11 stone chimneys were still standing, though the buildings had long since been burned. The remains of the old fort were still visible at the time of writing, especially the ruins of the chimneys.

Just Passing Through

There is another eastern access point to the Rockies a short distance north of the Bow River: Devil's Gap. On his 1841 world tour, HBC Governor Sir George Simpson and his entourage became the first white men to enter the mountains through Devil's Gap. This large party, with a pack train of 45 horses and 25 men, proceeded along the northern and western shores of Devil's Lake (Lake Minnewanka) that August. Simpson wrote:

> In the morning we entered a defile between mountain ridges, marching for nine hours through dense woods. This valley, which was from two to three miles in width contained four beautiful lakes, communicating with each other by small streams; and the fourth of the series, which was about fifteen miles by three, we named after Peechee as being our guide's usual home.[16]

Travellers approaching the mountains from the east passed through this gap in the mountain range (Devil's Gap) to approach the first of the three Ghost Lakes, shown in the foreground.

They continued past Cascade Mountain and along the banks of the Bow River through present-day Banff, following the old Native pony trail between Old Bow Fort and Laggan. After having travelled only a short distance along the Bow, the party headed south at today's Brewster and Healy creeks (the Sunshine Village access road) and continued on toward Simpson Pass. Despite the brevity of this initial visit to the Banff area, Simpson is hailed as Banff's first tourist.

That same year, another large party made an equally short visit to the Bow Valley. James Sinclair, a leader of the Red River Métis, guided 23 Métis families (116 people) and two hundred head of cattle to the Oregon Territory (present-day states of Washington and Oregon). Sir George Simpson had instigated the trip in hopes of reinforcing British claim to the disputed territory, thus ensuring the continuation of the HBC's trading privileges in the area. Simpson instructed Sinclair to use the well-known fur-trade route over Athabasca Pass.

Sinclair, however, had his own ideas, preferring to try a new pass to the south and perhaps gain the honour of having it named after him. He followed Simpson from Edmonton to Devil's Gap then deviated from his superior's route by following the south shore of Lake Minnewanka

Above: Sir George Simpson, governor of the Hudson's Bay Company between 1826 and 1860, was one of the first non-Natives to enter the mountains through Devil's Gap. He was the first to comment on the four lakes that followed the gap: the three Ghost Lakes and Lake Minnewanka.

Below: Red River Métis James Sinclair led a party of settlers from the Winnipeg area to Oregon's Pacific Coast.

Above: The trail along Carrot Creek, used by James Sinclair, requires many creek crossings. The reason for this becomes clear when viewing the sheer rock wall in the centre of this photo.

Below: White Man Gap, shown here with the second of the Grassi Lakes in the foreground, was the route James Sinclair used to take his large party of settlers toward White Man Pass.

to an Aboriginal trail over Carrot Creek Summit and on to the Bow Valley. Led by Wetaskiwin Cree Chief Maskepetoon, Sinclair and his party followed the old Native pony trail east along the Bow to the site of present-day Canmore. The large and cumbersome party crossed the Bow slightly west of The Three Sisters and headed south through White Man Gap (between the east end of today's Mount Rundle and Ha Ling Peak). They crossed the Continental Divide through White Man Pass and proceeded to the Columbia River, which they followed, reaching the coast by late fall.

Imperial concerns were also a motivating factor in the next recorded use of White Man Pass. In 1845, four years after Sinclair's initial crossing, British Army Lieutenants Henry J. Warre and Mervin Vavasour disguised themselves as gentlemen of leisure out for a round of hunting and fishing. Led by Peter Skene Ogden, a chief factor with the Hudson's Bay Company, the two were actually on a secret mission for the British Army, investigating the possibility of troop transport across the mountains. They used the trail along the Bow from Old Bow Fort to present-day Canmore, where they turned south to enter White Man Gap. Their only recorded comments on the area were that the surrounding mountains appeared magnificent but were covered by the smoke of an immense forest fire.[17]

Mere weeks later, Jesuit missionary Father Pierre Jean de Smet approached the summit of White Man Pass from the west. Having spent many years with the Aboriginal peoples of the Oregon Territory, de Smet had been instructed to extend his work to the Blackfoot bands east of the mountains. Upon entering the Bow Valley at present-day Canmore, he encountered a Stoney camp. He travelled with the band at least as far as Cascade Mountain, where he noted that "a beautiful crystalline fountain issues from the centre of a perpendicular rock about five hundred feet high, and then pours its waters over the plain in foam and mist."[18] He decided to retrace his steps east along the Bow to Old Bow Fort then continue on to Rocky Mountain House along the foothills.

Wesleyan Methodist missionary Reverend Robert Rundle was first led along the foothills to the Bow River by a band of Stoneys in 1841. At that time, Rundle had little interest in entering the mountains. But he returned to the area in late 1844, determined to explore. On November 7, he and his Stoney companions passed Old Bow Fort to enter the mountains on a snow-covered trail along the Bow. Two days later, Rundle attempted to climb his first mountain. It is not known which peak he attempted, but it was likely one of the lesser peaks along the route.

Rundle returned to the Bow Valley in 1847. After a difficult crossing of the Bow east of Old Bow Fort, he and his guides followed the river into the mountains. The guides led him to Lake Minnewanka, which he described as the most interesting lake he had ever seen. He carved his initials – RTR July 1, 1847 – in a tree before exiting the mountains through Devil's Gap at the east end of Lake Minnewanka.[19]

Bighorn rams feeding on early spring grass at the west end of Lake Minnewanka. Sheep are commonly found around the lake.

Jesuit missionary Father Pierre Jean de Smet entered the Bow Valley through White Man Gap after having crossed White Man Pass. He travelled very little in the Bow Valley.

Reverend Robert T. Rundle (1811–1896)

Robert Rundle was born in Mylor, England, on June 11, 1811. Religious vocations seem to have run in the family: his grandfather was a Methodist lay preacher and his uncle an ordained minister. Rundle himself became active in the Wesleyan Methodist Church at an early age. In 1839, two years after entering a Cornish business school, he was called to the ministry.

Only two months of training preceded his ordination as a Methodist minister. Eight days later, he left England for North America, where he was to serve as a missionary for the Hudson's Bay Company's Saskatchewan District. He landed in New York then travelled up the Hudson River to Montreal and on to Norway House (Manitoba) by canoe. Several months later, he proceeded to Fort Edmonton, the centre of the Saskatchewan District, where he arrived on October 18.

HBC Governor George Simpson's personal instructions that Rundle be treated with every kindness greatly eased the missionary's introduction into fur-trade society. He spent the next eight winters around the fur-trading posts of Fort Edmonton, Lesser Slave Lake and Fort Assiniboine, travelling by dog cariole and wearing heavy clothing to protect him from the elements.

In the spring, summer and fall months, he travelled through southern and central Alberta on horseback. A guide or HBC officer and a translator normally accompanied him on these journeys to visit First Nations at or near Rocky Mountain House, Pigeon Lake, Battle Lake and Gull Lake. Rundle's fondest memories of this time were of his visits with the Métis, Cree and Assiniboine around Rocky Mountain House and Gull Lake.

Rundle did venture farther south into Blackfoot country once and twice entered the Rocky Mountains: in 1844 and again in 1847. These forays into the Rockies resulted in a mountain

Rev. Robert Terrill Rundle.
(1811 - 1886)
First Protestant Missionary in North West Canada.

Opposite: Reverend Robert Rundle, who briefly entered the mountains along the Bow in 1844 and 1847, had the mountain between Canmore and Banff named in his honour, although he did not climb it.

Above: Mount Rundle extends from Canmore to Banff and is a major landmark in both communities. This image is taken from the east end of Canmore.

between present-day Banff and Canmore being named after him. Today, Mount Rundle is one of the best-known mountains in the region.

Throughout Rundle's North American posting, his primary goal was to convert the Aboriginal peoples to Christianity. He prioritized religious camp meetings over establishing mission stations or carrying out his duties as HBC chaplain. He had no energy for the Aboriginal mission school or the agricultural station near Fort Edmonton that the HBC pressed him to establish. He did eventually select a site for a school at Pigeon Lake, but he left it to his successor to actually begin construction.

In July 1847, Rundle fell from a horse and seriously injured his arm. The break did not heal properly, and in the fall of 1848, he decided to return to England to seek medical attention. He never returned to North America. He and Mary Wolverson married in 1854 and had nine children. Rundle served several English parishes until his retirement in 1887. He died on February 4, 1896, in Garstang, England.

In 1854 James Sinclair returned to the Bow Valley with a party of one hundred Métis from the Red River district, and, with 250 head of cattle, they made for the mouth of the Columbia River. This time, he intended to head south along the Kananaskis River and so chose Old Bow Fort as his access point to the Bow Valley. The party travelled by Red River cart to the fort then paused to transform the carts into pack saddles for the oxen's journey through the mountains. They and their new equipment followed the trail a very short distance west along the Bow. They crossed at the mouth of the Kananaskis River then turned south. After one false start, they eventually crossed North Kananaskis Pass. It was a long and very difficult trip to the coast, which probably left Sinclair wishing he had stuck with his previous route.

The "Lake of the Bow," as seen looking west from the Lac des Arcs Campground, is one of the first impressive mountain views that visitors see when driving west along the Trans-Canada Highway.

The Palliser Expedition

In August 1858, the ruins of Old Bow Fort witnessed a group of explorers and scientists about to determine the future of today's Western Canada. The British government and Royal Geographic Society had tasked Captain John Palliser, James Hector, Eugene Bourgeau, John Sullivan and Lieutenant Thomas Blakiston with establishing whether or not the HBC's Rupert's Land holdings were suitable for settlement and discovering if roads and railways could be built through the mountains. With respect to the latter, the Palliser Expedition had a specific mandate to explore all passes through the Rockies between the international border and the fur traders' Athabasca Pass.

Palliser decided to divide the group, asking Hector to explore to the north while he headed south. Palliser and his party left Old Bow Fort on August 18, travelled a very short distance west along the Bow and then forded it to follow Sinclair's route south along the Kananaskis River. A week earlier, geologist, naturalist and medical doctor James Hector,[20] botanist Eugene Bourgeau, Métis guide and interpreter Peter Erasmus, Stoney hunter Nimrod and two other Métis men named Brown and Sutherland had left Old Bow Fort with eight horses to thoroughly explore the Bow Valley.[21]

Hector and his party set up their first camp beside a string of lakes that Bourgeau named Lac des Arcs or Lake of the Bows. From there, Bourgeau also named Pigeon Mountain on the south side of the river. Another mountain farther south was named Windy (Wind) Mountain. (It was renamed Mount Lougheed in 1928.) After discovering a large cave while climbing a mountain on the north side of the river, Bourgeau and Hector named Grotto Mountain. Shortly thereafter, having briefly explored the area around Lac des Arcs and collected a large number of alpine botanical specimens, Bourgeau decided not to accompany Hector farther into the mountains. He lingered in the area for a while then returned to Edmonton.

Hector and his remaining companions continued along the old Native pony trail through the Bow Valley. Unlike previous easterners, he did not simply pass through the area; he carefully observed and documented its geology, flora and fauna.

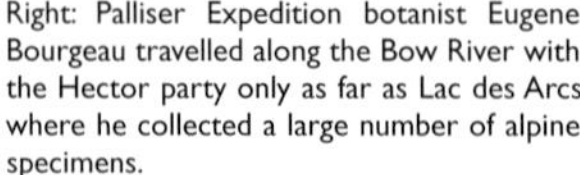

Above: Peter Erasmus, son of a Danish man and an Ojibwa mixed-blood woman, was a man of many talents who became a legend within his own lifetime.

Right: Palliser Expedition botanist Eugene Bourgeau travelled along the Bow River with the Hector party only as far as Lac des Arcs, where he collected a large number of alpine specimens.

His party's second camp was in the spot known today as Indian Flats, in the east end of Canmore. "Towards evening," Hector wrote in his diary, "an excellent camping place was reached opposite a mountain with three peaks, which forms a very imposing group. In a nearby clearing we made camp and stayed for several days making a geological study of the rock formation."[22]

This is the first recorded description of The Three Sisters, a well-known landmark along the Bow. At one time, the mountain was known as The Three Nuns. One unconfirmed story has it that a brother of railway engineer Major Rogers "looked out of the tent [one morning and] noticed each of the three peaks had a heavy veil of snow on the north side and ... said to the boys, 'Look at the Three Nuns'. They were called the Three Nuns for quite a while but later were called the 'Three Sisters,' more protestant like, I suppose."[23] In 1886 the geologist George Dawson officially named the peaks The Three Sisters.

Nimrod spent the second day in the Three Sisters area hunting to replenish the party's food supply while Hector climbed a peak northeast

Above: The waterfall on Cascade Mountain, first reported by Hector 150 years ago, has a subterranean source. The mountain was named in its honour.

Left: The foreground in this picture of The Three Sisters is Indian Flats, near where Hector and Rogers would have camped and possibly where the name The Three Nuns originated.

of the campsite. He named its range the Fairholme Range after Captain Palliser's sister, who had married William Fairholme in 1853.

The party then continued up the valley to the base of "The Mountain-where-the-water-falls," a translation that Hector abbreviated to Cascade Mountain.[24] The party set up camp at its base, and then Hector sent his men on ahead to clear a trail while he and Nimrod explored. Their journeys resulted in the first written description of three of Banff's most noted landmarks: Bow Falls, Tunnel Mountain and the Vermilion Lakes. "With Nimrod I set off to see a fine fall on the river, which lay about three miles out of the direct course," Hector wrote. "A high hill stands out in the centre of the valley, and it is in breaking past this that the river is compressed into a very narrow spout-like channel, and then leaps over a ledge of rocks about 40 feet in height ... above, ... the river is dilated and sluggish, and the valley is filled up with large swampy lakes."[25]

Hector also climbed Cascade Mountain in order to gain a better understanding of its geology and, having been informed by local Aboriginal peoples that Reverend Rundle had been in the area, named Mount Rundle in his honour. To this day, Bow Valley folklore would have it that Rundle actually climbed "his" mountain. There is no doubt that Rundle would have seen the mountain, since it extends along the Bow River all the way from Banff to White Man Gap near present-day Canmore. However, there is no written record of him travelling in the Banff area, and the fact that his journal makes no mention of Cascade Mountain or Bow Falls suggests that Rundle most likely used the only other route to Lake Minnewanka: along Carrot Creek and over Carrot Creek Summit. In spite of a 1911 account of Rundle's supposed climb published in the Methodist missionary magazine *The Foreign Field*, it is very unlikely that Rundle did climb the mountain.[26] Nevertheless, the name remains a valid tribute to one of the area's early travellers.

Proceeding with his own journey up the Bow Valley, Hector observed that "[a]long the eastern side runs a wall of vertical beds, of light grey limestone, the serrated edges of which at once suggested the name of Sawback Range for them."[27] The party continued as far as a peak Hector named Castle Mountain. In 1946 the name was changed to Mount Eisenhower to honour a World War II military leader, but public pressure provoked a return to its original name in 1979. Like The Three Sisters and Cascade Mountain, Castle Mountain is an obvious and well-known landmark to all people travelling in the Bow Valley. It was there that Hector's 1858 exploration of the Bow Valley ceased. His party turned southwest at this juncture, forded the Bow and headed over Vermilion Pass.

Opposite above: Tunnel Mountain and the Town of Banff as seen from the Sulphur Mountain Trail. Bow Falls is just left of where the river turns sharply around Tunnel Mountain. The Vermilion Lakes are to the left (not in the photo). Lake Minnewanka is in the background.

Opposite below: The west end of Castle Mountain, taken from the Castle Lookout trail, shows the rugged nature of this castle-shaped mountain. In 1946 this landmark along the Bow was renamed Mount Eisenhower in honour of World War II general Dwight D. Eisenhower. Public outcry resulted in the name being changed back to Castle Mountain in 1979.

The Allure of Gold

Early the following summer, the Bow River trail witnessed a new breed of traveller: men with their sights set on gold. Most gold seekers attempting an overland route to central British Columbia's Fraser River gold strike travelled west from Edmonton, crossing the Continental Divide at Yellowhead Pass. But a small number attempted the passage via southern passes; it was these Overlanders who headed for Old Bow Fort in the summer of 1859.

The nine men known as the Goodrich–Hastings party left Edmonton on June 9. Three days later, they crossed paths with Hector who, upon hearing that they intended to cross the mountains without a guide, gave them a map of Palliser's route over North Kananaskis Pass. Arriving at Old Bow Fort on July 1, the party joined forces with four other Overlanders. Like most others before them, they spent very little time in the Bow Valley, travelling west only to the mouth of the Kananaskis River, where they forded the Bow and headed south. Their crossing of the divide was difficult but successful.[28]

The second party of Overlanders, known as the New Brunswick party, was much larger than the first, numbering 45 men. At Old Bow Fort, they prepared to cross the mountains by breaking up their carts and wagons. Under the guidance of a Métis named Whitford, the New Brunswick party made excellent time and crossed North Kananaskis Pass without any difficulty.

Shortly after the New Brunswick party vacated Old Bow Fort, Hector was back, this time intent on following the old pony trail the entire distance from Old Bow Fort to the Pipestone River, where the village of Laggan (Lake Louise) would later be established. He and his party took advantage of the cart fragments the New Brunswick party had left strewn around the fort to repair their pack saddles, and then they retraced the previous year's journey. They camped at Lac des Arcs on August 18 and reached Castle Mountain on the 20th. This time, they

James Carnegie, Earl of Southesk, travelled through the mountains for pleasure and the pursuit of large game. He and Hector's party nearly crossed paths in the Bow Valley.

continued upriver to the junction with today's Pipestone River before leaving the Bow Valley, heading northeast along the Pipestone River and over Pipestone Pass.[29]

With this journey, Hector gained the honour of being the first recorded white man to travel along the Bow River from its entrance to the mountains to present-day Lake Louise. By pure coincidence, his feat was repeated less than two weeks later by explorers travelling in the opposite direction.

While Hector and his party were crossing Pipestone Pass, James Carnegie, Earl of Southesk, was laboriously making his way toward the Kootenay Plains at the end of a summer-long hunting trip in the mountains. Once on the plains, Southesk took what he called the Bow River Road (the old Native trail over Pipestone Pass and on to the Bow Valley). On September 2, near Hector's Castle Mountain, Southesk saw a tree blazed: "Exploring Expedition. Aug. 23, 1859. Dr. Hector."[30] In the wilds of the Front Ranges of the Rocky Mountains, the first two white men to travel in this area had missed each other by a mere ten days!

Upon reaching Laggan, the Earl of Southesk traded horses with a band of Stoneys and purchased food from them. He then proceeded down the old pony trail along the Bow, camping at the base of "the mountain where the water falls" (Cascade Mountain). The party arrived at Old Bow Fort on September 30, 1859, relieved to be out of the mountains. Finding the remains of carts left behind by the New Brunswick party and the Palliser Expedition, Southesk's men used the discarded outfit to craft three complete carts and harnesses to facilitate the remainder of their journey to Edmonton.[31]

A third party of Overlanders, the seven-man Caldwell party, had left Edmonton on September 20. On October 4, they met up with the Earl of Southesk northeast of Old Bow Fort. The meeting was beneficial for both parties. The Overlanders were able to trade salt, flour, rice and dried apples for tobacco, fresh meat, a moose skin and a shoeing hammer. One of Southesk's men even shod several of their horses for them. But, more important, Southesk was able to arrange for one of his Stoney guides to lead the Overlanders, who had been unable to find a guide before leaving

Edmonton, through the mountains. His skilled leadership enabled the party to cross the mountains without any difficulty.

Two years later, Dr. Alexander P. Reid and four Overlanders arrived in Edmonton looking for a mountain guide. They eventually hired Baptiste Gabriel, an Assiniboine Métis, and left Fort Edmonton on September 2, 1861, with their sights set on gold. A mere 11 days later, somewhere north of the Bow River in the foothills of the Rockies, Gabriel deserted, taking two horses with him. The men knew they were ill-equipped to proceed alone yet felt they could not turn back. They pressed on, hoping they would recognize the Bow when they came to it and somehow find the route to North Kananaskis Pass.

The party successfully reached the Bow River a few days later. But even after sending two men 15 miles (24 kilometres) upstream, they could not find a ford that would allow them to proceed to the pass. As they struggled to determine their next steps, two Aboriginal men miraculously appeared on the scene. They managed to surmount language barriers well enough to ask how to best cross the mountains, at which point one of the Natives offered to guide them.

Rather than crossing the Bow and heading toward North Kananaskis Pass, the guide continued up the river, following Hector's trail past Mount Rundle and along the wide valley of the Sawback Range. On the third day, they reached a large Stoney camp near Castle Mountain. The chief informed the Overlanders of the route over Vermilion Pass, which they successfully followed to make their way down the Vermilion River, through Sinclair Pass and on to the Columbia River. Before reaching the Columbia, the guide left, taking one of their best horses in addition to the other horse, blanket, buffalo robe, gun and powder he had requested as pay. With great difficulty and a modicum of good luck, the party eventually made it through the mountains.[32]

Today's Highway 93 can be seen leading to Vermilion Pass on the left of the photo. Early travellers would have followed parallel to Altrude Creek, visible to the left of the highway.

Railway and Towns

After this final Overlander party passed through, 18 years passed without any recorded activity in the Bow Valley. Though there were certainly Aboriginal peoples travelling through the area, the old pony trail along the Bow would likely have become overgrown and barely visible. But it was not to remain so for long. The events at the conclusion of the third period of exploration irreversibly transformed the Bow Valley from a relatively pristine wilderness area to a national transportation corridor. The Canadian Pacific Railway (CPR) would pass through the valley, with permanent settlement springing up in its wake. Local industries would naturally follow, primarily coal mining to supply the railway, and outfitting, hotels and other establishments to supply the growing tourist industry.

The changes all began in 1879 when John Macoun, survey naturalist with the Geological Survey of Canada, arrived in the Bow Valley. Until then, the railway had been scheduled to run north through Edmonton, crossing the divide over the relatively low Yellowhead Pass. But in 1879 and 1880, Macoun explored the southern prairies as far as the Bow River. He travelled up the river past Old Bow Fort and at least as far as Cascade Mountain, where he viewed the future site of Banff.[33] These explorations, which probably took place during wet years, convinced him that the southern prairies were not the semi-desert reported by Palliser and others. He made it his mission to convince the railway builders of the agricultural potential of the area. And while the railway executive committee's dramatic change of plans is still a poorly understood aspect of Canadian history, Macoun's assessment of the region undoubtedly played a role.

However the Canadian Pacific Railway's route was ultimately chosen, its construction ushered in a period of dramatic change for the Bow Valley. By 1881 the scouts and surveyors under Major A.B. Rogers, engineer in charge of the mountain division of the CPR, had passed Old Bow Fort to reach the gap near the present-day town of Exshaw. Rogers and his assistant, Tom Wilson, soon to become the first and most famous of the Bow Valley pioneer outfitters, herded a pack train up the valley, cutting and

John Macoun (1831–1920)

A pompous young man, John Macoun was known throughout his life for his optimism and unbounded enthusiasm, which often led him to overstate his case. He felt strongly that Canada, with its unlimited resources, should become the home of a superior civilization where immigrants like him could start with nothing and make a good life for themselves.

John Macoun was born in Northern Ireland on April 17, 1831. He became fatherless at the age of six, and, perhaps as a consequence, developed a stubborn and independent streak. Indeed, he became almost self-righteous in his determination to succeed. At the age of 19, he and his family immigrated to Upper Canada (Ontario) and it was there, in the open fields and forests, that Macoun developed his lifelong interest in botany. Dissatisfied with farming, he became a public school teacher in 1856 and on January 1, 1862, married Ellen Terrill of Brighton, Upper Canada.

Shortly before their marriage, Macoun had secured a position in Belleville. The move would profoundly transform his life. Amidst a growing family, which eventually included two sons and three daughters, he devoted every spare moment to botany, developing a herbarium and rapidly becoming an expert on the flora of the region. In 1868 his efforts were rewarded with an appointment to the chair in natural history at Belleville's Albert College.

"The Professor," as he became known, specialized in field work. He was obsessed with collecting specimens, choosing to leave the difficult work of identification and classification to others. Unfortunately, his annual field trips were often little more that haphazard sweeps through a region, and because he relied on others to identify his specimens, his collections sometimes sat around for years before being classified.

Professor John Macoun was a botanist, explorer and naturalist who travelled widely in Western Canada, collecting specimens for the Geological Survey of Canada.

A chance 1872 encounter with Sandford Fleming led Macoun to undertake an extensive survey along the proposed route of the railway. Between 1872 and 1881, Macoun crossed Canada several times, examining the agricultural potential of various western tracts. Although others very knowledgeable in the field severely criticized his conclusions, Macoun's contagious enthusiasm swayed government policy-makers.

His overly optimistic assessment of the potential of what had become known as the "Palliser Triangle" lands in southern Alberta and Saskatchewan undoubtedly contributed to the rerouting of the Canadian Pacific Railway from the Yellowhead Pass to Kicking Horse Pass. As a result, many new settlers suffered undue hardship, and, ironically, Macoun's overzealous enthusiasm ultimately undermined federal homestead policy.

Macoun's work for the railway survey also caught the attention of the Geological Survey of Canada; he was named dominion botanist to the survey in 1881. The following year he moved his family to Ottawa, where he continued his feverish collecting activity. Macoun's belief that the role of the naturalist was to assemble a complete inventory of the natural wonders of his nation, including all living things, decisively influenced the Geological Survey's approach to natural science.

Macoun was a prominent figure in Ottawa's social and intellectual circles for over three decades. He became a charter member of the Royal Society of Canada in 1882 and was often seen visiting the Governor General's residence. He gave talks to both literary and scientific societies, and his home was often a centre for intellectual discussions. In 1886–87 he served as president of the Ottawa Field Naturalists' Club.

Macoun's field work, presentations and social activity came to an abrupt end when he suffered a stroke in 1912. His wife was no longer well either, so the two decided to move to Vancouver Island to live with one of their daughters. Macoun managed to continue limited work with the Geological Survey for the remainder of his life and also worked on an autobiography called *Autobiography of John Macoun, Canadian Explorer and Naturalist, 1831-1920,* published in 1922 by the Ottawa Field Naturalists' Club. He died on July 18, 1920.

In spite of the weaknesses of his methodology, John Macoun attempted to single-handedly roll back the natural-history frontiers of Canada. His belief in himself and his work led the Geological Survey to consider natural history a legitimate concern, and his enormous collections led to the formation of what became the National Museum of Canada.

widening the old Native pony trail as they went.[34] At Bath Creek (west of today's Lake Louise), the party turned west toward Kicking Horse Pass, the chosen route for the railway.[35]

Earlier that year, the base camp for railway work had been established southwest of Old Bow Fort, near the mouth of the Kananaskis River. Local workers named the place Padmore after F.W. Padmore, the popular assistant commissary of the CPR. The community is considered the first permanent settlement in the Bow Valley.

Materials made their way to the region in several stages. First, the I.G. Baker Company of Fort Benton, Montana, used pack horses and freight wagons to transport materials from Fort Benton to Old Bow Fort. From there, local jack-of-all-trades David McDougall ensured their safe arrival in Padmore. In 1882 Tom Wilson was hired to pack supplies from Padmore up the Bow Valley to the survey crews in the Kicking Horse valley. He and fellow packer Johnson Stevenson travelled with strings of 14 to 16 pack horses for ten to 12 days round-trip to get the supplies to the crews.

The Bow Valley's silence had been permanently disturbed. Survey crews worked its length, blazing trails and cutting lines. Other workers were busy clearing and widening pack trails and tote roads to allow packers through with equipment and supplies.[36] It didn't take long for the trail up the Bow to become a well-worn track. CPR Engineer-in-Chief Sir Sandford Fleming travelled along this route in 1883, observing the progress of the surveyors as far as the summit of Kicking Horse Pass.[37] However, before leaving Calgary, Fleming had been unable "to obtain any reliable information of the country through which we had to pass."[38]

By 1885 the area between Old Bow Fort and the top of Kicking Horse Pass – which a few years earlier was marked only by a pony trail – was home to a completed railway line that formed an integral part of a national transportation system. In 1886 the first transcontinental passenger train chugged along the old Indian trail.

Along with the trains came the towns. As construction had progressed, sidings or stations had been built, numbered consecutively west from Medicine Hat (Siding 1). Siding 27 was established as a divisional point,

where trains could be serviced and crews changed. A round house for the service work and living quarters for the operating crews were established, as at all divisional points. After the depot was completed in 1884, Siding 27 was renamed Canmore, after King Malcolm of Canmore, Scotland. Coal was discovered that same year, and within three years, Canmore had become a thriving mining town. Coal continued to be mined there for the next 92 years.[39]

After the railway's completion in 1885, its very first settlement, Padmore, was abandoned. The centre of population moved farther west, and the name changed to Kananaskis.[40] By 1887 the booming community was already home to at least 30 people and had a sawmill, limestone quarry, railway station, water tower and section house.

West of Canmore, near where the Cascade River emptied into the Bow, another coal-mining town quickly grew at Siding 28. By 1887 Anthracite had three hundred permanent residents, but poor coal quality forced the mine to close in 1897, rendering Anthracite a ghost town.

Siding 29, complete with section house and log station, was built a short distance along the line at the base of Cascade Mountain. A few log buildings soon sprang up, and the siding was renamed Banff to recognize the birthplace of CPR president George Stephen in Banffshire, Scotland. In 1887 three hundred people resided in the townsite west of Siding 29 and another 50 near the station. In 1888 the railway decided to move the station to the present site of Banff, and the old log structure was moved from Siding 29. The people living at the old station site soon moved to the new Town of Banff, and by 1897 Siding 29 had disappeared.

The vagaries of industry were not the only threat to these pioneering towns. An unusually heavy snowfall over the winter of 1883–84, for example, followed by very warm temperatures in the spring of 1884, led to severe flooding. The snow melted so quickly that the river channel could not contain the deluge. The overflow caused major property

Best known for his toughness and unparalleled proficiency with foul language, Rogers is honoured today for his discovery of the pass that bears his name.

Above: Coal was discovered in Canmore (Siding 27) in 1884. The town grew up on both sides of the river: "townside" and "mineside." This 1907 image shows the "mineside" area, south of the river.

Right: The coal-mining town of Anthracite (Siding 28) grew up at the junction of the Cascade and Bow rivers, near the base of Cascade Mountain, in 1887. Ten years later, the mine (located in a ravine captured on the right side of this photo) closed and Anthracite became a ghost town. Today the area is overgrown, and the course of the river altered. The townsite's former location is marked by the Cascade Power Plant and surge tower.

damage in the fledgling towns along the Bow. Roads along the bank were inundated and houses swept away. One report indicates that Anthracite "saw a number of houses all crushed together and torn from their foundations by the force of the water in the Bow."[41] The water's maximum height was recorded at the railway station and "appeared to have covered the rail road tracks to the depth of several feet."[42] Nearly 20 years later, in 1902, the Bow flooded again, shutting down the railway for six days and inflicting damage that required major repairs to roadways along the river.

Sandford Fleming (1827–1915)

Sandford Fleming was an exceptionally talented man of humble beginnings. He was born on January 7, 1827, at the Scottish industrial town and seaport of Kirkcaldy. He obtained a preliminary education in science and technology before leaving for Canada at the age of 18, where he quickly became involved with Canada's fledgling railroads. He worked as chief engineer of the Northern Railway in Ontario and the Intercolonial, which ran between Quebec and Halifax.

One of Canada's primary railway builders, Fleming was among the first to suggest a railway to the Pacific Coast. He was fittingly named chief surveyor for the Canadian Pacific Railway in the 1870s and oversaw much of the surveying across the prairies and through the mountains. Although his favoured route to the coast, the Yellowhead Pass, was rejected in preference for the more southerly Kicking Horse Pass, it was later used by the Canadian Northern Railway. He retired from the CPR in 1880.

Although most of his working life was associated with railways, Fleming was also an engineer, scientist, explorer, designer and author. A vigorous explorer, he crossed Canada more than once during his lifetime, using all means of transportation available to him (foot, snowshoe, dog team, canoe and wagon). He published a book on railway inventions in 1847 followed by one on the international railway in 1876. He was also responsible for designing Canada's first postage stamp, the three-penny beaver, which was issued in 1851.

Fleming devoted much of his writing to promoting ideas that were extremely influential both in Canada and around the world. In 1878 he began publishing papers advocating a system for international standard time. By 1883 all North American railways had adopted his system, and by the early twentieth century, it had been universally adopted. For many years, he worked on a proposal to link Canada and Australia by cable. His book, *Canada and British Imperial Cables*, was published in 1900; the telecommunications cable across the Pacific was laid in 1902.

Fleming received many awards over the course of his lifetime, including a knighthood, but the honour that brought him the most satisfaction was his appointment as Chancellor of Queen's University in Kingston, Ontario. He served the position with distinction for 35 years. When he died in Halifax on July 22, 1915, Canada lost a truly great achiever.

Sir Sandford Fleming was an extremely gifted man who served as engineer-in-chief for the construction of the CPR. He is perhaps best known today as the person who invented international standard time.

By the time the railway reached Castle Mountain in 1884, the boom town of Silver City had sprung up. Back in 1881, Joe Healy, an Irish-born American prospector, had a piece of ore analyzed and found it to be fairly high in silver. He returned the following year to investigate further, and word soon spread. By 1884 Joe Smith, who had pioneered settlement at Silver City before the boom, had built a rooming house and a pool hall. Two hotels, several saloons and the Royal Northwest Mounted Police barracks – established to enable them to keep order among the nearly three hundred inhabitants – rounded out the town's amenities.

In 1884 explorer and mountaineer Professor A.P. Coleman stopped in Silver City during his summer's adventures. This was Coleman's first trip to the mountains; on subsequent trips, he discovered Fortress Lake and solved the "David Douglas controversy" of Athabasca Pass.[43] En route to Silver City in 1884, he stopped to see his brother in Morley and met David McDougall, who asked him to look at a claim he had staked behind Castle Mountain in Horseshoe Valley. While he was there, Coleman made the first recorded ascent of the mountain. He then rode the railway to the end-of-steel at Laggan and continued on the old tote road to the Selkirks.

By 1885 hopes for a significant ore strike had diminished and Silver City became a ghost town almost overnight. When English minister William Spotswood Green visited Silver City resident Joe Smith in 1888, "[t]he empty log houses were empty shells, the streets were grass grown and the station had little other than the water tower to supply the locomotives. Two section men and their wives had a house they used, but of the prospectors and miners there were no signs."[44] Joe Smith stayed on, living in a small house until he moved to the Lacombe Home in 1937, where he died shortly thereafter.[45]

Early in the twentieth century, another town sprung up on the old pony trail between Old Bow Fort and Laggan. By 1907 the town of Exshaw, just west of the old settlement of Kananaskis, boasted about 20 buildings as a result of the cement plant that had been built there a few years earlier.

Above: Siding 29, the original site of the Town of Banff, grew up near the base of Cascade Mountain, close to where the airstrip is today.

Left: Joe Smith, the bachelor hermit of Silver City, settled before the boom and stayed on another 52 years after the town disappeared. As Smith got on in years, residents of Banff and Lake Louise who passed by would make sure smoke was rising from his chimney – a sign that all was well.

Below: In 1884 the boom town of Silver City grew almost overnight at the base of Castle Mountain. It died almost as quickly the following year.

Unlike other towns along the railway, Exshaw (shown here in 1908) was neither a railroad town nor a mining town. Its economic base is cement manufacture, and the town continues to thrive.

Pony Trail to Auto Road

The completed railway supplanted most other means of travel between Old Bow Fort and Laggan (Lake Louise Station) – the starting point of most pack-train travel to the North Country. Still, the old tote road did see some use. In July 1890, the Reverend Charles W. Gordon arrived in Canmore to take charge of parishes in Banff, Canmore and Anthracite, as well as any lumber camps in the area and the railway points as far west as Field. Gordon travelled back and forth through the area year round, sometimes by train but more often on horseback. He later achieved international fame as an author, publishing approximately 30 novels under the name of Ralph Connor, many of which drew heavily from his life as a frontier minister in the Bow Valley and elsewhere.[46]

In the summers of 1891 and 1897, John Macoun returned to Banff in order to make a representative collection of the flora and fauna of the newly formed Rocky Mountains Park. These trips would have enabled him to see for himself the changes he had precipitated.

In the summer of 1893, Tom Wilson, now establishing himself as the region's foremost outfitter, had Stoneys William and Joshua Twin[47] and their families trail a small herd of horses 80 miles (129 kilometres) from Morley to Laggan along the railway tote rode so that a group of wealthy easterners – including Mary Schäffer and her husband, Charles – could ride the three miles (five kilometres) from Laggan Station to Lake Louise.

At that time, the occasional visitor was still travelling by wagon from Calgary to Banff along the old tote road. West of Banff, only saddle horses travelled the trail once the railway was completed; in 1904 it was referred to as a bridle (pony) path.[48] Construction on a coach road from Calgary to Banff began in 1907 and was completed in 1909. But it was 1913 before cars were allowed into the town and, even then, not after dark. Improvements to the old bridle path west of Banff began in 1911. The westward push continued each year, and by 1915 a good gravel road extended as far as Castle Mountain.

Road-building efforts were given a boost that year when nearly 200 detainees from World War I enemy countries were transferred from the Lethbridge internment station. By July 19, the Castle Mountain internment camp contained 191 men who were immediately set to work on the road. All work was done by hand, using picks, shovels and wheelbarrows. The men were often hungry and unhappy and took every opportunity to escape. In November they were moved to winter quarters near Banff. They returned to Castle Mountain in late June 1916 to complete clearing and gravelling 11 miles (18 kilometres) of roadway. By the spring of 1917, the Banff camp had been closed and all road-building projects were terminated.[49] The remainder of the road to Lake Louise was not completed until 1921.

By 1916 legislation had changed to allow cars throughout Banff National Park. As roads improved, automobile travel became an important means of access to Banff and Lake Louise, and public campgrounds were built to accommodate motoring tourists. Rocky Mountains Park's first gatekeeper, Annie Staple, was hired in 1916. The park's eastern boundary at that time was near Exshaw. As there were no other facilities, a table and tent were set up near the road. During Staple's lengthy career, the park gate moved from Exshaw to Carrot Creek (west of the present location) then to the present location just east of Carrot Creek.

Even as these developments proceeded, a few enthusiastic trail riders like Dr. Charles Walcott, secretary of the Smithsonian Institute, continued to travel on horseback.[50] Walcott was a workaholic geologist-palaeontologist who spent 18 summers collecting fossils and studying the geology of the Canadian Rockies.

Because he owned his own horses and outfit, Walcott could not simply travel to Laggan by rail as most other travellers did. In 1916, for example, he wintered his horses in Shelby, Montana. On June 19 he, his wife, Mary, camp manager and cook Arthur Brown, and wrangler Alex Minton, headed north with a dozen horses, a wagon for freight and a new buckboard (a lightweight wagon usually fitted with springs and seats). Averaging a tough 30 miles (48 kilometres) a day, they had passed through Calgary by July 3 and continued to follow the Bow River past Old Bow Fort and on to Banff. After exploring the Mount Assiniboine area, they returned to Banff then followed the newly completed automobile road to Castle Mountain and the tote road on to Lake Louise, arriving there on August 8.

Above: The Twin brothers, William and Joshua, were Stoneys who cleared trails and carried out other tasks in the early days of settlement in the mountains. Much of their work was for the CPR, but in this case they were working for outfitter Tom Wilson. They had strong ties with the Brewster family of Banff.

Opposite above: Internees from the Castle Mountain internment camp helped build the motor road from Banff to Lake Louise during World War I. Workers shown here are using hand tools only.

Opposite below: Black bears foraging for food along the Bow Valley Parkway (the old pony trail between Banff and Lake Louise) are an exciting sight for tourists but often lead to traffic jams.

In 1917 the Walcott party again used the road and trail to ride from Banff to Lake Louise and on to Kicking Horse Pass before returning to Banff at the end of the summer. Walcott commented that the string of horses had to share the road with autos. In fact, two years later, he found that the automobile road had taken all the grass, forcing his horses to graze near the railway tracks. In 1921 the 71-year-old Walcott commented that the 34-mile (55-kilometre) buckboard ride from Banff to Lake Louise was a long trying trip due to the heat and dust. The following year he complained that rough spots along the motor road made the trip tedious. (If it was rough for a horse-drawn buckboard, imagine what it was like for

Annie Staple, the first gatekeeper for Rocky Mountains Park, continued to work at the park entrance through its three relocations over the course of her lengthy career.

Charles William Gordon (1860–1937)

Charles William Gordon – best known today by his nom de plume, Ralph Connor – was born on September 13, 1860, at Indian Lands Presbyterian manse, Glengarry County, Ontario. His father, Donald (Daniel) Gordon, was a Scottish Presbyterian missionary, and his mother, Mary Robertson, was the daughter of another Scottish Presbyterian missionary. Gordon grew up enjoying the backwoods of Ontario with his sister and five brothers. His early education took place in public schools in rural Ontario and at St. Mary's in Harrington, Ontario.

After high school, he worked for a year earning enough money to attend University of Toronto in 1880. There he was active in sports and music, forming the Toronto University Student Quintet with his brother, Gilbert, and three friends. After graduating from the University of Toronto, Gordon again worked for a year before beginning theological studies at Knox College, Toronto. By 1887, when he and the other four members of the quintet had finished their studies, their music was highly in demand in Toronto. All five then embarked on a long-time dream to attend the University of Edinburgh, where their music also became extremely popular. They spent the following year (1888–89) touring Europe on bicycles before returning to Toronto, where the group disbanded.

Gordon assisted his father in his ministry until 1890, when his mother died and he accepted an appointment at a mission field headquartered at Banff but including the mining towns of Anthracite and Canmore.

A year and a half later, Gordon declined a call from an established Winnipeg church, preferring to continue his work amidst the miners and railway workers in the Bow Valley. Two years later, another call came from Winnipeg, from his old minister and friend from University of Toronto days, Dr. J.M. King, who was

Reverend Charles Gordon, known widely as Ralph Connor, the author of romantic accounts of life in the North-West, was an accomplished musician and dedicated Christian minister.

now principal of Manitoba College. This time Gordon accepted the call, becoming the first minister of Winnipeg's St. Stephen's Presbyterian Church, where he stayed until his 1924 retirement. During his stay in Winnipeg, he met and later married King's daughter, Helen. The year of their marriage is uncertain, but they did have one son and four daughters.

It was Gordon's dedication to home mission work in the mountains that started him on his writing career. He began writing his fictionalized accounts of life in the North-West in an attempt to raise public awareness and money for the mission. His exciting romances received instant popularity and success. Most of his novels were written between 1899 and 1914.

At age 54, Gordon enlisted as chaplain of the 43rd Cameron Highlanders and was posted overseas. In 1916 he was recalled to Canada to promote the Allied cause in the United States. The wartime death of his friend and financial advisor, Colonel R.M. Thompson, led to the loss of most of Gordon's personal fortune and also an accumulation of debt – which he forbade family members to discuss. After the war, Gordon became very active in a variety of social issues, including church union, politics and international relations. He also attempted to resume his writing career, only to discover that the popularity of his romantic fiction had peaked. Nevertheless, he continued to write, devoting much of his later work to social themes, such as unemployment. He received several awards later in life, including an honorary doctorate from the University of Glasgow. He began his last major writing project, an autobiography, in 1936, but he did not finish it before his death the following year.

Although Gordon was considered one of the country's most popular early-twentieth-century authors, and study of his works continues among students of Canadian literature, Gordon always remained somewhat detached from his literary career, considering his first role in life to be that of a Christian minister.

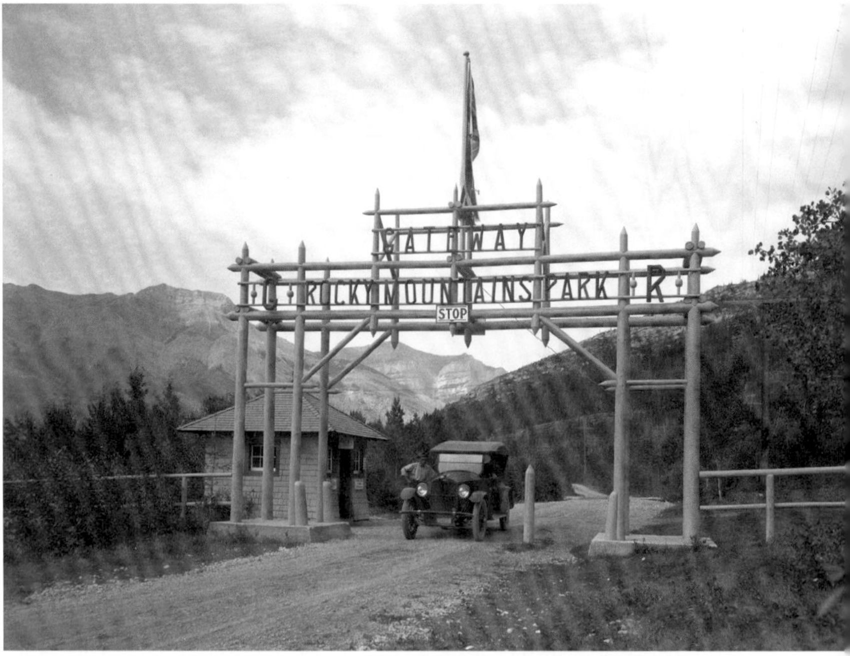
GATEWAY
C ROCKY MOUNTAINS PARK R
STOP

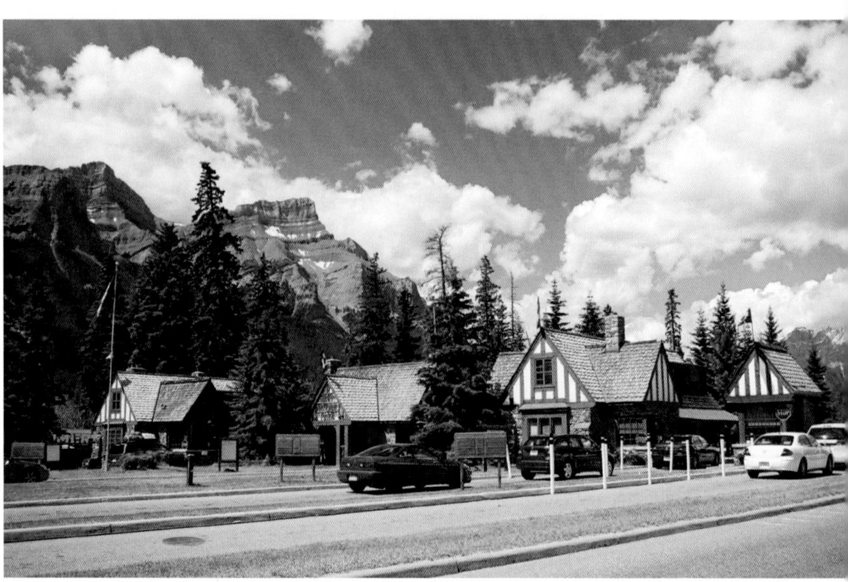

cars!) This was the last time he travelled the road by buckboard. In future years, he opted to travel by train to Lake Louise or Field and let his men bring the outfit to him.[51]

On July 2, 1933, the motor road between Banff and Lake Louise was witness to a most unusual procession. Cliff and Ruth Kopas had been married on the morning of June 17, 1933, in Okotoks, Alberta. Later that same day, they set off on a four-month, 1,500-mile (2414-kilometre) honeymoon pack-train trip to Bella Coola, British Columbia. Twenty-three-year-old Ruth, who had never before ridden a horse, had agreed not only to marry Keith but also to help her 22-year-old mate fulfill his childhood dream of crossing the mountains on horseback. Ruth's philosophy was the same as that of her Biblical namesake, "Whither thou goest, I will go."[52] As they progressed along the trail, Ruth became an expert at handling horses and was not only Cliff's companion and first true love, but his biggest supporter.[53]

The young couple owned five horses and had $2.65 in cash. Their route took them through the foothills to Kananaskis Country then along Spray River and Bryant Creek to Mount Assiniboine. From there, they continued west through the Valley of the Rocks to Sunshine Meadows and along Healy Creek to the Bow River. They headed upstream along the Bow on the motor road, hoping to reach Lake Louise by July 1, where Ruth's family was to meet them and help celebrate Ruth's birthday. As they travelled along the road with their five-horse pack train, they "presented an attraction for motoring tourists almost equal to a bear or a moose alongside the road."[54] By the time they reached Lake Louise, they were a day behind schedule, and as they were completing the last leg of the trip, they were "overjoyed to be discovered by Ruth's folks, traveling in a pickup truck."[55] At camp that day, "great piles of

Opposite above: A 1921 view of the eastern entrance to Rocky Mountains Park, near Exshaw, where Annie Staple, a widowed warden's wife, acted as 24-hour gatekeeper. The G and R on the sides of the gate stand for "George Rex," King George V.

Opposite below: The eastern entrance to Banff National Park has expanded considerably since 1930, when it was moved to close to its current location, and is a very busy spot during the summer months.

food appeared out of the truck and were eaten," a more than welcome feast for the frugal honeymooners.[56]

After two days exploring around Lake Louise, the couple headed north on the old pony trail toward the icefield (see Route II below).

Between 1881 and 1921, the pony trail from Old Bow Fort to Laggan (Lake Louise) had been transformed into a cart track, and then a railway and finally an auto road. The final transformation came in 1959, when the Trans-Canada Highway (mainly on the south side of the river) was completed to Lake Louise, and the original road on the opposite side became Highway 1A. In the first decade of the twenty-first century, the Trans-Canada between Castle Junction and Lake Louise was widened into a four-lane divided highway, with fences on either side to keep animals off the road and overpasses and underpasses to allow animals access to the other side of it.

Fencing of the Trans-Canada Highway through Banff National Park decreases animal mortality but overpasses, such as the one shown here, and underpasses must be provided to allow animal movement across the highway.

The Trail Today

Old Bow Fort, the starting point for the trail along the Bow to Laggan, sits on a high plateau northeast of the mouth of Old Fort Creek at the Bow River. The surrounding area is very open, offering a full view of the river in both directions. Although we do not know what may have grown there at the time the fort was built, there is no longer any obvious source of trees for construction.

Unfortunately, there is no hiking or bicycle trail that would allow non-motorized travellers to retrace the original pony trail from the fort to Lake Louise. Highway 1A approximates much of the route, but although some cyclists do use it, the highway is not particularly bicycle-friendly. The road is narrow and the section between Exshaw and Canmore is heavily used by large trucks. Beyond Banff, the 1A sees a great deal of tourist traffic in the summer. The abundance of giant motor homes and absence of shoulders make this a particularly hazardous route for cyclists.

Near Old Bow Fort, Highway 1A is some distance north of the Bow River. The original trail probably descended a deep ravine to a suitable crossing point of Old Fort Creek before heading west. Just west of the Highway 1X intersection near Seebe, the old trail would again have run close to today's 1A. In fact, highway construction likely obliterated most of the old trail. A provincial government signboard on Canmore's Grassi Lakes trail indicates that two small sections of the old pony trail still exist: one on a high bench just north of Lac des Arcs and another just north of Gap Lake. Between Gap Lake and Canmore, the present-day Highway 1A and the railway both follow close to the river, likely on top of portions of the old pony trail.

Just east of Canmore, the Trans-Canada Highway crosses to the north side of the Bow River. This highway, the railway and the 1A travel parallel to one another through the town until Highway 1A disappears just west of town. It reappears near the western exit to the town of Banff. The old pony trail along this stretch likely disappeared with construction of the four-lane divided Trans-Canada Highway.

After crossing toward Banff at the overpass on the western Banff intersection, a right turn leads onto the Vermilion Lakes Road. This road is part of the old 1A and likely also part of the old pony trail. It parallels the Trans-Canada to the end of the Vermilion Lakes, where it is interrupted by the main highway crossing to the south side of the river. It is not possible to continue on the 1A with an automobile, but pedestrians and cyclists can follow a path under the highway to reconnect with the 1A at the Fireside Picnic Area.

After the Fireside Picnic Area, the 1A, now called the Bow Valley Parkway, follows the railway along the north bank of the Bow River to the village of Lake Louise. The route likely follows the original pony trail (and later wagon road) fairly closely; the narrow road and low speed limit make for pleasant driving. The route offers several good views of the Bow Valley and its riverside marshes. It also contains a number of burned-out areas – the result of prescribed burns. Picnic areas are set out along the route, as are signboards describing the area's features, including the sites of Silver City and the World War I internment camp. Tourist facilities include campgrounds, chalets and various short hiking trails along non-historic routes.

A view east along the Vermilion Lakes, with a portion of the old highway shown on the left, running along the lakeshore. The four-lane Trans-Canada Highway is above the old road, on the left.

Trail Guide

Distances are adapted from existing trail guides: Patton and Robinson, Potter, and Beers, and from Gem-Trek maps. Distance intermediate from those given in the sources are estimated from topographical maps and from hiking times. All distances are in kilometres.

Old Bow Fort to Lake Louise

Maps 82 N/8 Lake Louise
82 O/2 Jumping Pound Creek
82 O/3 Canmore
82 O/4 Banff
Gem Trek Canmore and Kananaskis Village
Gem Trek Banff and Mount Assiniboine

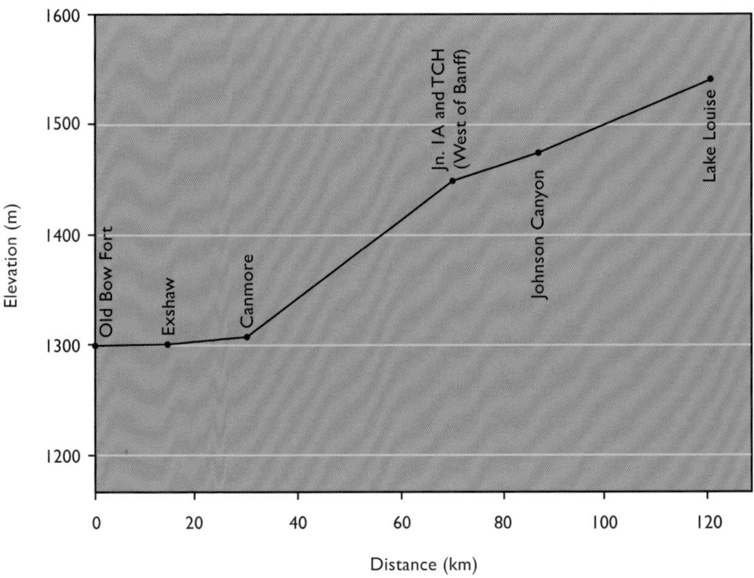

Trailhead

To reach the site of Old Bow Fort, proceed east on Highway 1A from Canmore. Approximately 6 km east of the Seebe turnoff (Highway 1X), Highway 1A crosses a small creek. This is Old Fort Creek. Continue on the 1A for about another 4 km to a gravel road leading to the right (south). The remains of the old fort are at the junction of Old Fort Creek and the Bow River. Because this site is on the Morley Reserve, you will need permission from the Morley band to visit the site. Phone the Stoney Tribal Administration office in Morley for permission and instructions.

0.0 The entire Old Bow Fort–Lake Louise trail is now a road. The Trail Today section above (page 77) provides a guide to travelling Highway 1A and the Trans-Canada Highway to Lake Louise, approximating the route used by early travellers before the highways were built.

The Bow Valley Parkway is likely close to the route followed by Hector in 1859. When driving this route, watch for game, such as this bull elk grazing near the parkway.

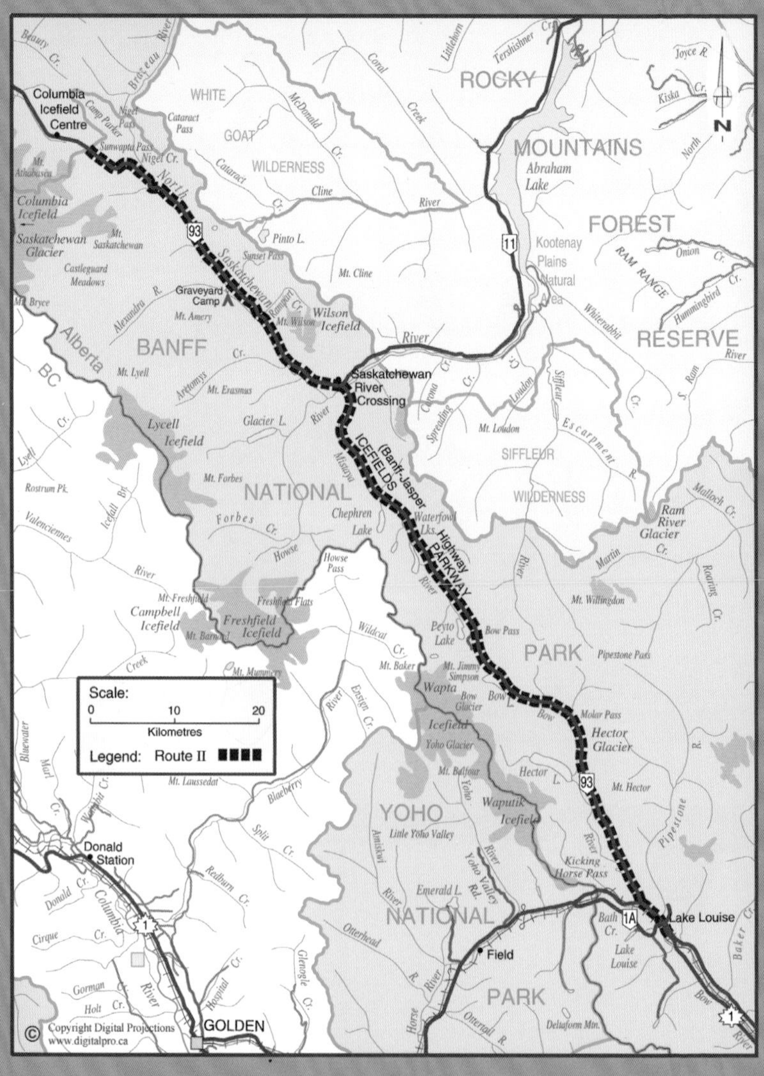

The historic trail from Laggan (Lake Louise) to Sunwapta Pass (Columbia Icefield).

Route II

Muskeg, Lakes and Passes: Laggan to Sunwapta Pass (Columbia Icefield)

It was the summer of 1893. Jimmy Simpson had accepted a contract to cut a trail from Laggan to Bow Lake for the Canadian Pacific Railway and had hired Jim Tabuteau and Frank McNichol to assist him. A mess of fallen timber and repeated river crossings stood between the determined men and their destination. But the sight they beheld upon reaching the lake redeemed every second of toil. Simpson declared it "the most beautiful thing I'd seen in Canada."[1] And the best was yet to come. When they proceeded to the north end of the lake, Simpson fell in love with the location and declared: "I'll build a shack here sometime."[2] Twenty-five years later, he started building his lodge. Paying guests began arriving as early as 1934; six years later, the lodge, named Num-Ti-Jah after the pine martin that was so prevalent in the area during Simpson's trapping days, was substantially complete.

My wife, Cheryl, and I recently had the privilege of staying at the lodge. Although it is no longer operated by the Simpson family, we were delighted to find that Jimmy Simpson's presence can still be strongly felt. Lawn chairs invited guests to linger with the view out over the lake and Bow Glacier to Mount Jimmy Simpson. Simpson's original residence, the

Above: In 1893 Jimmy Simpson declared Bow Lake to be the most beautiful thing he had seen in Canada. It is framed by the massive Crowfoot Mountain on the left and the Bow Glacier to the right of centre.

Opposite: In the 1930s Jimmy Simpson built Num-Ti-Jah Lodge near the north end of Bow Lake. The octagonal design was employed to keep the walls short, as building materials had to be brought from Lake Louise by pack horse.

"Ram Pasture," was still in good condition and scheduled for an upgrade. The old corrals he and his son had used in their outfitting days could still be explored, and the skiing and hiking were the same as ever.

Indoors, photographs of the "old days," stuffed heads from wild animals Simpson hunted and works of art adorned the walls. Collecting works from such notable painters as Carl Rungius, Belmore Brown and Charlie Russell, Simpson amassed one of the finest art collections in Western Canada. In his later years, he took up painting, selling his works to lodge visitors and, in 1958, to the Glenbow Foundation.

Furthermore, the managers' ability to recreate the Simpson family's famous friendly atmosphere created an exemplary experience. Late in the afternoon, large trays of delicious hors d'oeuvres were served in the sitting room, where guests could mingle. These were followed by a gourmet dinner, served *en famille* in the dining room. After dinner guests were again invited to mingle in the sitting room and enjoy additional sweet tidbits as they gazed out over the surrounding peaks. It was hard for a history-loving guest to leave without recognizing that Jimmy Simpson was indeed one of the greatest pioneers in the Canadian Rockies.

Chronology

1858 Hector and his men continue north along the Bow River and on to the North Saskatchewan River. This historic trip is the first time non-Natives are recorded to have crossed from the Bow River drainage to that of the North Saskatchewan.

1887 Tom Wilson escorts two English sportsmen, H.W. Calverley and Arthur Brearley, along the Bow and Mistaya rivers to the Howse Pass and Kootenay Plains areas.

1895 Charles Fay, Philip Abbot and Charles Thompson of the Appalachian Mountain Club walk almost as far as Bow Lake with guide Tom Wilson. The mountaineers climb Mount Hector.

Walter Wilcox and guide Bill Peyto travel north along the Bow as far as Bow Summit. They explore the area around Bow and Peyto lakes.

1896 Bill Peyto takes hunters Peabody and Barns up the Bow from Laggan to an area north of Bow Lake. They cross Bow Pass on September 21.

1897 Charles Fay, Charles Thompson and fellow climber Herschel Parker join up with Norman Collie, George Baker and Harold Dixon to travel up the Bow to the Bow Lake area, leaving Laggan on August 7. Bill Peyto guides them.

Later that year, Baker and Collie return north with Swiss guide Peter Sarbach for another month of climbing in the Howse Pass area.

Americans Stanley Washburn and friend arrive in the mountains, prepared for a hunting and fishing expedition. Guide Fred Stephens agrees to lead the two greenhorns, who make it only partway up the Bow Valley.

1898 Tom Wilson hires Jimmy Simpson to cut a trail from Laggan to Bow Lake.

Wilcox returns to Bow Summit with Bill Peyto as guide. They continue down the Mistaya to the North Saskatchewan River.

Jimmy Simpson escorts a Miss Brunstermann and noted Canadian historian Agnes Laut through the muskegs of the Bow River trail as far as Hector Lake.

1899 Jimmy Simpson and Fred Ballard are sent north to clear the trail from Bow Summit down the Mistaya River to the North Saskatchewan.

Head guide Ralph Edwards and neophyte cook Jimmy Simpson lead two English hunters, Messrs. Parker and Twyford, up the Bow to the Wilcox Pass area.

1901 Fred Stephens guides Stanley Washburn and companions north from Laggan to the Columbia Icefield.

1902 Bill Peyto, assisted by Jimmy Simpson and Fred Ballard, guides Reverend James Outram and Swiss guide Christian Kaufman as far north as the junction of the Athabasca and Alexandra rivers, where the party turns west.

Fred Stephens guides Norman Collie and his English mountaineering comrades, Hugh Stutfield and Hermann Woolley, American climber George Weed and Swiss guide Hans Kaufmann north along the Bow to climb in the Glacier Lake area.

1903 The Department of the Interior assigns A.O. Wheeler the task of surveying along the Bow Valley between Laggan and Bow Pass, using the Bow River trail as the access road.

Fred Stephens guides Stanley Washburn and companions on a second attempt to reach the Yellowhead Pass. Again, they make it only as far as the Columbia Icefield.

1906 Billy Warren guides Mary Schäffer and Mollie Adams north from the Kootenay Plains to the Columbia Icefield. They return along the Bow.

1907 Billy Warren and Sid Unwin guide Mary Schäffer and Mollie Adams up the Bow River, into the Athabasca River drainage and along the upper reaches of the Athabasca to Coleman's Fortress Lake.

Jimmy Simpson escorts the butterfly lady, Mrs. Mary de la Beach-Nichol, from Laggan to the Wilcox Pass area, where they happen to meet up with Mary Schäffer's party.

1910 Jimmy Simpson, with packer and cook Ernie Brearley, returns to the Wilcox Pass area, again with a very interesting customer: wildlife artist Carl Rungius.

1911 The Alpine Club of Canada holds its annual camp in the Consolation Valley, near Lake Louise. After the camp, a group of 11 attendees take part in a six-day expedition up the Bow Valley to Bow Lake.

1912 The Warden Service builds a trail from Laggan to Bow Summit, a distance of 30 miles (48 kilometres).

1913 Canadian climber J.W.A. Hickson, travelling with Swiss guide Edward Feuz and outfitter and guide Ernie Brearley, leaves Laggan for the Howse River area on August 6.

1916 John Wilson leads his sisters Bess and Slats (Dora) and friend Jen along the Bow River to the North Saskatchewan and east to the Kootenay Plains to visit the old homestead where their father, Tom Wilson, spent several winters.

Jimmy Simpson, cook Watty Failes and wrangler Bob Alexander escort hunters Robert Frothingham and George Martin from Lake Louise north to the North Saskatchewan River.

1918 Geologist and palaeontologist Charles Walcott and his wife, Mary Vaux Walcott, head up the Bow Valley toward Lake Louise. They continue on to the north end of Bow Lake, where they, camp manager Arthur Brown and packer Alex Mitten set up a base camp.

1919 Caroline Hinman and her Off the Beaten Track tour travel up the Bow Valley from Laggan to Nigel Pass.

1923 Jimmy Simpson begins building his shack on the north shore of Bow Lake, the beginnings of Num-Ti-Jah Lodge.

In early August, Bill Potts guides climbers J.W.A. Hickson and Aime Geoffrion and Swiss guide Edward Feuz north to the Alexandra River, where they turn west toward Thompson Pass. They are followed by J. Monroe Thorington later that year.

1925 Caroline Hinman and her Off the Beaten Track tour use the Bow Valley route to return from a long summer of travel in the Rockies. They reach the North Saskatchewan via the Alexandra River.

1926 Several groups of mountaineers head up the Bow Valley for climbing outings in the Howse Pass and Castleguard Meadows areas.

1929 Jim Brewster provides an outfit for Leopold Amery to climb Mount Amery near the Alexandra River. The mountain had been named after him two years earlier.

1931 The road between Banff and Jasper is begun as a Depression make-work project.

1940 The road between Banff and Jasper is officially opened as the Banff–Jasper Highway.

1941 Dr. Albert Wiebrecht, with family and friends from Milwaukee and Chicago, hire mountain guides Edward Feuz and Ken Jones to lead a mountaineering trip near Howse Pass.

1961 The road between Banff and Jasper is improved and paved, and its name is changed to the Icefields Parkway.

History

The Trail to the North Country

Toward the middle of the nineteenth century, British leaders, fearing for the security of their western North American holdings, tasked Captain John Palliser with assessing the lands' suitability for railways and settlement. Palliser and his team spent the first year of their expedition crossing the prairies, and then they devoted the summer of 1858 to alpine exploration.

On September 8, having just returned from the first non-Aboriginal exploration and crossing of Kicking Horse Pass, expedition physician and natural historian James Hector was keen to locate Howse Pass before winter set in. Through intermittent snow storms, he and his party (see Route I above) followed the Bow River to a large lake (Hector Lake). The cold weather encouraged them to camp winter-style. The adventurers built a large fire surrounded by pine boughs, and then, wrapped in their blankets, they arranged themselves in a circle, with their feet toward the fire.

James Hector of the Palliser Expedition was the first non-Aboriginal man to cross from the Bow River drainage to that of the North Saskatchewan. All of the expedition's explorations north of the Bow were done by Hector and his party. The unfortunate kick Hector received from his horse, which led to the naming of the Kicking Horse River, did not slow him down.

They resumed travels the following day, catching good views of the glaciers that sit atop the Continental Divide. They continued on past Bow Lake and Bow Summit then started down the Mistaya valley. The lack of reference to Peyto Lake in Hector's journal suggests that the party did not see it. They set up their second camp by today's Waterfowl Lakes then continued on to the North Saskatchewan River, thus accomplishing the first recorded crossing from the Bow River drainage to that of the North Saskatchewan.[3]

Though Hector makes no mention of a trail, the Stoney people are known to have travelled to the Kootenay Plains along that route, so he and his men were likely following an old Stoney trail. Aboriginal peoples had been travelling through the Rockies for millennia, and the Bow, Mistaya and North Saskatchewan rivers provided an obvious northward route. Even when a trail was not visible to early non-Aboriginal travellers, stacks of tepee poles, fire rings and other markings often bore witness to prior use.

Nevertheless, the route between Laggan and the Columbia Icefield held little appeal to early explorers from the East. The first of these travellers – men affiliated with the fur trade – had little interest in actually exploring in the Rocky Mountains. Their driving motive was to cross the Continental Divide to access the lucrative fur-bearing animals in British Columbia. The nearest these men came to travelling the Laggan–Icefields corridor was when David Thompson and Joseph Howse and their men crossed from the North Saskatchewan

Coyotes can be seen along the Icefields Parkway, although they are often more difficult to spot than other wild animals since they blend in with the grasses.

River to the Howse River (today's Saskatchewan Crossing) en route to Howse Pass.[4]

Between Hector's exploratory trip and the completion of the railway in 1885, the Bow–Mistaya River route to the north continued to be used almost exclusively by Native bands. Even once the completion of the railway ushered in the fourth period of exploration, most early mountaineers and explorers stayed close to Laggan and Field.

A few hunting parties did, however, make the northward journey – including the group with whom Tom Wilson launched his guiding and outfitting career. Wilson had spent a summer with a group of Stoneys; their travels included retracing Hector's trip to the North Saskatchewan then proceeding east to the Kootenay Plains.[5] So when English sportsmen H.W. Calverley and Arthur Brearley arrived in Laggan in 1887, eager to hunt big game, Wilson agreed to take them to the Howse Pass and Kootenay Plains areas. They headed north along the Bow with three saddle horses and two pack horses.[6] Unfortunately, as neither guides nor hunters tended to record their exploits, no other details of the trip are available, and no other excursions along the Bow were recorded for almost ten years.[7]

Later in his career, Tom Wilson established a trading post on the Kootenay Plains. He is shown here in front of the cabin where he lived alone for several winters.

Pioneering Mountaineers and Adventurers

One of the first parties to record their travels along the Bow River trail left Laggan in July 1895. Appalachian Mountain Club members Charles Fay, Philip Abbot and Charles Thompson were keen to climb in the Canadian Rockies. Abbot explained that:

> Our first step was to get hold of Wilson the best guide and outfitter for that region, and to hold a council of war. Many plans were proposed, but none hit our fancy. Finally, for about the tenth time since he joined us, Thompson brought forward his fixed idea. Mt. Hector was reasonably near to Laggan, ... but not too near; it had never been climbed; better still, it had been attempted without success; and it was high, because the Canadian surveyors, when they turned back, had already reached 10,400 feet. It further appeared that Wilson himself had been with that party; and he said he believed the peak could be climbed.[8]

There being no horses available at the time, the party resorted to accessing their peak by foot. Mountaineers often walked to condition themselves for the climb ahead, but their porter, "a taciturn and admirably patient individual named Hiland" got the worst of the deal.[9] "Each man carried his own blankets ... and the provisions were equitably divided." Hiland was left carrying "an enormous and shapeless pack composed of the tin things and all the other articles which the rest of [the party] refused to touch."[10]

The challenging trail was criss-crossed with fallen timber. After a long day of swamps and mosquitoes, the climbers thought they had reached a point where they could turn east to the mountain, only to find that Wilson "had camped the time before at the shore of Bow Lake, only a little way ahead" and wished to return.[11] His clients yielded and tramped on.

> Six o'clock came, then seven, then eight, and no sign of the lake. The sun had set, and the mosquitoes were so thick that [they]

> could hardly see one another. About half-past eight Wilson said that the lake was still nearly half a mile away.... That settled it.... It was half-past ten before [they] had finished supper, untwisted and stretched [their] rope, got things together for the morning's start, and [they] were ready to turn in.[12]

Thankfully, their fortunes improved. After successfully scaling Mount Hector the following day, they returned to camp to find that Hiland had prepared a delicious dinner of fresh mountain trout. Wilson waited to ensure that his clients returned safely from their climb, offered some quick instructions on crossing the Bow and then hurriedly departed to tend to other business back in Laggan. Eager to investigate the icefield to the west, the climbers made a valiant attempt to cross the Bow River. Thwarted, they retraced their route to Laggan the following morning.

The Appalachian Mountain Club members were not the only adventurers to head north that summer. Tom Wilson had also shared word of the Bow Lake region with Walter Wilcox. On August 14, 1895, Wilcox headed north with guide Bill Peyto, a cook and five horses. "Not far from the station," Wilcox explained, "there commenced an old tote-road, which runs northward for many miles, towards the source of the Bow River.... Thus for several miles we enjoyed easy and rapid travelling...."[13] A few miles along the route, they "came to the house of an old prospector. As this was the farthest outpost of civilization and the old man was reported to be an interesting character, I entered the log-house for a brief visit.... In a state of solitude and absolute loneliness ... this man had spent several years of his life, and, moreover, was apparently happy."[14]

Appalachian Mountain Club member Philip Abbot, recognized as one of the foremost mountaineers in the United States at that time, was the first person to die in a climbing accident in the Canadian Rockies. His ill-fated ascent of Mount Lefroy took place in August 1896.

Walter Wilcox was one of the first non-Aboriginal people to explore the route north from Laggan to Bow Summit and Sunwapta Pass and the Athabasca drainage. The route he followed around the Athabasca Glacier bears his name. Wilcox spent many summers in the Canadian Rockies, exploring as far south as the Mount Assiniboine area. He is shown here with (l–r) Stoney John Hunter and outfitter Tom Wilson.

This easy travelling, however, was soon interrupted by what guide Ralph Edwards had earlier reported as "one of the most universally detested stretches of trail in the Rockies."[15] Travelling south, Edwards found that:

> From just below the Lower Bow (Hector) Lake to within a few miles of Laggan the trail (such as it was) ran through a gigantic blow-down. Many years previous the area had been devastated by a great forest fire, which had destroyed all green timber for several miles along the old trail.... [T]he burnt timber was being continually blown down by every successive windstorm, but there was still much left standing.... [T]he trail was continuously blocked by fallen, or leaning trees, crisscrossed in every direction.... Every outfit passing that way had more or less trail cutting to do, depending on how much wind there had been since the last party went through ...[16]

Wilcox and his party spent two trying days pushing through this detestable stretch of trail to Bow Lake. Camping in view of the great glaciers, however, refreshed both bodies and spirits. The following day, at the top of Bow Pass, Wilcox caught his first glimpse of what he called the Saskatchewan River (today's Mistaya River).

> I shall never forget the first view we had into the valley of the Saskatchewan [Mistaya]. Approaching a low ridge at the south side of the valley, suddenly there is revealed a magnificent panorama of glaciers, lakes, and mountains, unparalleled among the Canadian Rockies for its combination of grandeur and extent. To the south, one beholds the end of an immense glacier [Peyto Glacier], at the termination of which there are two great arched caverns in the ice. From out of these issues two roaring glacial streams, the source of the Saskatchewan [Mistaya] River ...[17]

Through the forest, they could see a brilliant robin's-egg-blue lake far below. The lake was later named Peyto's Lake, since guide Bill Peyto was reputed to have left the crowds at Bow Lake to seek solitude at Bow Summit. The name was later shortened to Peyto Lake.

Wilcox went no farther on this trip, returning via the Sawback Range for a total of 23 days on the trail.[18] The following year, he repeated the trip to Bow Pass and continued on in hopes of reaching the Athabasca River drainage. In his account of the journey, Wilcox explained that "it was virtually impossible to obtain any information in 1896 and trails were essentially non-existent.... Proceeding north, [we] did not know whether to follow the Alexandra River or the North Saskatchewan in order to reach the Athabasca. On climbing a mountain, [we] could see the Alexandra River valley blocked by a glacier and carried on along the North Saskatchewan even though the canyons looked very deep."[19]

Despite the apparent depth of the canyons and difficulties of the trail, the Wilcox party proceeded without incident to the top of today's Sunwapta Pass, where the Athabasca Glacier blocked further progress. The

Above: Peyto Lake, taken from the viewpoint on Bow Summit, looking north down the Mistaya valley. The lake is named after Bill Peyto, a very capable but eccentric outfitter who is reported to have sought refuge here from the "crowds" around Bow Lake.

Below: The Fay party at Laggan in 1897. (l–r) Charles S. Thompson, Charles E. Fay, unknown, Harold B. Dixon (seated), unknown, unknown, J. Norman Collie (with pipe), Hershel C. Parker and Peter Sarbach. The unidentified men include A. Michael and C.L. Noyes.

continuation of the trip around the icy obstacle is described in the next chapter. The only other travellers who recorded journeys north of Laggan that summer were two hunters, Peabody and Barns, who had Bill Peyto guide them up the Bow to an area north of Bow Lake in mid-September.

By 1897 Appalachian climbers Charles Fay and Charles Thompson had sufficiently recovered from their miserable trail experience two years earlier to attempt another Rocky Mountain expedition. They and fellow climber Herschel Parker teamed up with three like-minded individuals from the English Alpine Club – J. Norman Collie, George Baker and Harold Dixon – to travel up the Bow toward Bow Lake and climb Mount Balfour. This time they hired Bill Peyto as guide, Lorne Richardson as packer and Charlie Black as cook. Swiss guide Peter Sarbach rounded out the party.

For some unknown reason, the outfitters made the unusual decision to set out ahead with half the party, leaving three ponies to be packed and trailed by Collie, Fay and Baker. Fay, of course, had travelled the route before, but none had significant backcountry experience. Had it not been for the assistance of a man at Laggan railway station, the greenhorns would not even have managed to pack all the gear on the ponies. Then began their adventure along "what for want of a better term was called the trail, but in reality consisted of a tortuous route over fallen trees, through willow thickets and into endless swamps or muskegs."[20]

Fortunately, Peyto had marked the trail, and if one inexperienced trail-finder strayed from the route, another was quick to spot a blaze. Bit by bit, they made their way through the mess of fallen timber only to find themselves immersed in the endless swamps of the open valley. More than once, the ponies sank to their bellies in muskeg. Making matters worse, Collie explained, "the 'blazes' stopped, and, following some upright sticks of wood (that we afterwards found had to do with the railway survey up the valley), the tracks of the other animals were soon missed, and we got lost."[21]

The sun set with horses and climbers still stuck in the muskeg. Fay decided to boldly push on, finally reaching the outfitters' camp about 11 o'clock. Meanwhile, just as the others had begun to fear they'd be spending the night in the muskeg, Peyto arrived to guide the men to camp. The unfortunate ponies, however, were consigned to spend the night in the swamp under the watchful eye of Peyto's dog.[22] Amazingly, the men were not deterred from their desire to climb. En route to Mount Balfour, they successfully scaled several smaller peaks. Balfour itself, however, proved beyond their abilities, and on the descent Thompson fell, head-first, into a crevasse. Lowered on a rope, Collie managed to rescue his inverted companion, without injury to either, and the ill-fated party returned to Banff.

The very next morning, Baker and Collie, with a month of holiday remaining, "were so fired with enthusiasm over the high rock-peak they had seen to the north-west from the summit of Gordon" that they decided to head back north.[23] Sarbach agreed to accompany them, and Wilson was able to provide the same outfit they had just used. They departed on

(l–r) Peter Sarbach, George Baker and J. Norman Collie relaxing in Banff before beginning their 1897 trip.

August 17 amidst sweltering heat and swarms of mosquitoes. The trail was as bad as ever, covered in deadfalls. Collie explained:

> It was early in the afternoon when Peyto announced that we should camp: to us this seemed unnecessary, so we told him so, but without any effect. Later, after dinner, ... he [said that] he was there to look after the horses and should camp where he considered best; ... [because] he was not going to have sore backs and lame horses in his outfit.... [W]e were out for a month, and it was no use quarrelling on the first day. That Peyto was right was abundantly proved in the sequel; for owing to the excessively hot weather, we soon had more than one pony with a sore back and ill.[24]

They reached Bow Pass on August 20, spent a day resting the horses and making survey measurements and then continued on down the Mistaya River to the Waterfowl Lakes (which they named for the large flocks of ducks on the lake waters). Three days later, the adventurers reached the North Saskatchewan, where they turned west up the Howse River to climb and explore in the Howse Pass area. They soon discovered that it was no

Opposite: An industrious beaver family has dammed the ditch and meadow area beside the Icefields Parkway. One family member is seen here carrying food to a winter stash.

Right: Just a few metres from the beaver pond along the Icefields Parkway, this grizzly was contentedly feeding, paying little attention to the line of camera-laden visitors along the road.

vain boast of Peyto's that he was there to look after the horses; many a time after arriving in camp after a long day's journey, when something to eat and drink was one's first thought, Peyto could be seen driving the sore-backed ponies down to the stream where he carefully washed them and smeared the raw places with bacon grease to deter the flies.[25]

After two weeks of travelling and climbing, they returned to the railroad via Howse Pass.[26]

Another novice to alpine travel and camping arrived in Laggan late that summer with a burning in his heart and a "lust for the mountains that has never yet been quenched."[27] Stanley Washburn and a friend were keen to hunt and fish; guide Fred Stephens agreed to lead them. The party set out northward along the Bow River, with Stephens riding and trailing a pack horse and the two other men on foot. "We did not think we were tender-feet," Washburn reported. "I suppose no one ever does. We had six-shooters, shot-guns, Rifles, hundreds of rounds of ammunition and enough fishing tackle to have eliminated all of the 'finny tribe' for ten square miles around."[28]

But after a mere four days, the two easterners insisted on going home. Stephens suggested returning along a different route, likely trying to prolong the outing. He proposed heading over a pass (probably Molar Pass) to the Pipestone then following it to Laggan. Once they reached the Pipestone River, Washburn took one horse and headed toward Laggan on his own. He managed to get lost but did eventually arrive at his destination – several hours late. Although his friend never returned to the mountains, Washburn was still enthusiastic.

He would have been pleased to learn that the condition of the Laggan to Bow Lake portion of the trail was considerably improved the following summer. Tom Wilson, on contract with the CPR, hired Jimmy Simpson to cut a trail to Bow Lake. Simpson was likely wishing he had cut it farther when he followed a trip to Emerald Lake by guiding a Miss Brunstermann and noted Canadian historian Agnes Laut through the muskegs of the Bow River trail to Hector Lake.[29]

Walter Wilcox did not benefit as much as he might have hoped either when he set his sights on Thompson's Glacier Lake that fall.[30] He, guide Bill Peyto, cook Roy Douglas and a complement of nine horses left Laggan on October 12, but late fall conditions meant that it took them six days to follow the Bow and Mistaya to the North Saskatchewan. Still, they managed to explore the Glacier Lake region before returning to Field over Howse Pass.[31]

A year later, in October 1899, Jimmy Simpson put his cooking skills to use helping Ralph Edwards guide two English hunters, Messrs. Parker and Twyford, along the Bow to hunt. They camped at Simpson's favourite site at the north end of Bow Lake then proceeded to Wilcox Pass, where game was reputed to be plentiful. Unfortunately, the area did not hold up to its reputation. The disappointed hunters returned home without even having spotted any game. Young Simpson, however, gained valuable experience in his burgeoning career; he eventually became one of the most respected hunting guides in the Rockies.[32]

Two years later, Stanley Washburn returned to Laggan fired up by the ambitious goal of travelling north to the Yellowhead Pass and down the Fraser River to the West Coast. Joining him were two companions nicknamed Pink and Ricky, Fred Stephens as guide, Frank Hippach as packer, John Scales as cook, six saddle horses and nine pack horses.

They left Laggan in July and, in spite of the fact that Simpson's cutting had considerably improved the trail since their previous trip, it took them four days, including some heavy chopping, to reach Upper Bow Lake. Washburn seconded Simpson's suggestion that the lake was "as beautiful a spot as a man can find in a seven years' journey in the mountains.... On the north end of the lake was a bit of timber, and in the shadow of these firs we pitched our tents."[33]

Glacier Lake was first viewed by David Thompson in 1807. Dr. James Hector named it in 1858. The accumulations of snow and ice that led Dr. James Hector to name it Glacier Lake in 1858 are clearly visible to the right of centre.

After a day's rest at the future site of Simpson's Num-Ti-Jah Lodge, Washburn and companions continued down the Mistaya River. It took five days of intense chopping to reach the North Saskatchewan. On July 21 they crossed the Mistaya River, where, "[o]ut on the little flat by the junction of the rivers, [Washburn] discovered an old stump, squared on four sides, on which was inscribed in blue keel, the name and date (1883) of one of the Canadian Pacific Surveys...."[34] They continued upstream along the North Saskatchewan and camped for two days while building a small raft to ferry their goods safely across the river.

"The next days," Washburn explained, "we spent in pushing our way up the north fork of the river, and a worse trail I had never encountered up to that time, for we were held up day after day in fallen timber, and by the horses getting into muskeg and mire."[35] It took a whole week to attain a point opposite Mount Wilcox at the Columbia Icefield. The party promptly set up camp and ascended Mount Wilcox to hunt. They managed to bag three bighorn sheep to supplement their dwindling food supplies. Washburn injured his ankle on the excursion, however, and had to spend two weeks recovering in camp. This unexpected delay exhausted their new food supply and pushed the party back to Laggan. Thus ended Washburn's first rather feeble attempt to reach the Yellowhead.

He returned to the Rockies two years later, still intent on reaching Yellowhead Pass. This time he was travelling with a mining engineer, a mountaineer and a doctor named August Eggers. They hired Fred Stephens as guide, a cowboy from Montana as packer and a man named Nat to cook. The trip was disorganized from the start. When the rest of the party was ready to leave, the mountaineer was busy climbing. The others set out up the Bow and down the Mistaya.

Jimmy Simpson and Fred Ballard had cleared the trees from Bow Summit down the Mistaya to the North Saskatchewan the previous spring, which increased the traffic on the trails, which in turn worsened the muskegs and bog holes, leaving the trails in their worst condition ever. Still, the party made it to the North Saskatchewan. Stephens settled the crew in camp then returned to Laggan to fetch additional supplies and the mountaineer. After ten long days of waiting, the remainder of the group crossed to the west bank of the Mistaya. They waited another two days before Washburn and Eggers decided the time had come to seek out the others. They found Stephens and the mountaineer a mere 12 miles (19 kilometres) back; all were reunited in camp the next day.

The reassembled party promptly set out on the trail, following the North Saskatchewan as far as the icefield. By then, the easterners had lost all desire to proceed on to the Yellowhead. Tired of travelling, they turned back toward Laggan. Fourteen days later they were able to rest their heads on fluffy hotel pillows.[36] Remarkably, Washburn did eventually make it to the Yellowhead in 1909 (see Route III below).

In the meantime, Reverend James Outram organized the first Bow Valley climbing party since 1895 not to include at least one mountaineer with prior experience along the route. Supported by the CPR, Outram left Laggan on July 9, 1902. Bill Peyto led the outfit, with assistance from Jimmy Simpson and Fred Ballard. Christian Kaufmann joined the team as climbing guide. They had ten fully loaded pack horses, four saddle horses and a ton (907 kilograms) of gear. Leaving Laggan, they joined up with Fred Stephens, who was trailing 15 horses and two foals to transport food and supplies to the Collie party at the junction of the North Saskatchewan River.

Peyto, who had other outfitting clients to attend to, travelled only as far as the North Saskatchewan River. He helped the outfit cross the river safely then returned to Laggan with three of the pack horses. Jimmy Simpson was left to begin his long and successful career as a trail guide. He led Outram up the Alexandra River to his main objective, Mount Columbia, which Outram successfully climbed.[37] During the 54 days Outram was on the trail, he participated in the first ascents of ten peaks and achieved all of his objectives. He arrived back in Laggan on August 30, three days after Norman Collie, Hugh Stutfield and Herman Woolley.[38]

Ever since the first signs of spring, these three British climbers had been dreaming of the Canadian Rockies, "[t]hose peaks and glaciers and canyons, and the subtle charms of camp-life in the backwoods, [which] had woven a spell around us that we could not, if we would, have broken."[39]

Fred Stephens promptly responded to their request for an estimate for a four-week trip. His proposal met with general acceptance – except when it came to food. Having run short of food on their previous expeditions, the mountaineers doubled their suggested rations and requested that half the supplies be cached at the junction of the Mistaya and North Saskatchewan rivers.

The climbers left England on July 3 and, after some delays due to lost luggage and one of their American friends being called home, arrived in Laggan late on July 23 – four days later than planned. Two of the packers, Dave Tewkesbury and Clarence Murray, had already left with the tents and other gear. The remainder of their party: American climber George Weed, Swiss guide Hans Kaufmann, guide Fred Stephens and cook Jack Robinson, were waiting to greet them.

The climbers proceeded north along the Bow the morning of July 24, finding the muskeg and bog holes worse than ever where the trail descended to the level of the river. They soon caught up with their packers; on July 28 the entire party arrived at their 1898 camp, where the food had been stashed. Stutfield explained that:

> Collie's first care was to search for two bottles, one of whisky, the other of brandy, which he had buried at the foot of a tree in 1898, with elaborate instructions as to how they were to be found. You stood, compass in hand, at the foot of a certain tree; then walked twenty-two paces north-west to another tree with a blaze on it; then twenty-five paces due north to a tree with a white stone at its base, under which the bottles were buried.... We ... had no difficulty in finding them, and copious libations from their well-matured contents were drunk round the camp-fire that evening.[40]

The party remained in camp the following day, likely to clear their heads of the effects of the previous evening's celebration. They forded the Mistaya River the morning of July 30 and headed west toward Glacier Lake and several weeks of adventure in the area of Mount Forbes and the Freshfield group. They returned along the Bow River trail near the end of August, reaching Laggan on August 27.

Alpine surveying involved a great deal of mountaineering, and surveyors were actively involved in founding the Alpine Club of Canada. Some of the founding group, shown here: (l–r, back row) unknown; Jack Otto, outfitter; A.O. Wheeler, surveyor, president; Tom Wilson, outfitter; S.H. Mitchell; R. Campbell, outfitter. (l–r, front row) Dan Campbell, outfitter; M.P. Bridgland, surveyor and chief mountaineer; unknown; Reverend J.C. Herdman; A.P. Coleman, explorer and mountaineer, vice-president.

The Surveyors

More than a decade passed before another mountaineering party travelled the Bow River route, but the trail was far from silent. In the summer of 1903, the Department of the Interior appointed A.O. Wheeler as one of its topographers and assigned him the task of surveying the Bow Valley between Laggan and Bow Pass.

Wheeler's brother, Hector, and Morrison Bridgland, a recent University of Toronto graduate who would go on to make his name as a Rocky Mountain surveyor and mountain climber, assisted him with his 1903 survey of the Bow Valley.[41] The department hired Jimmy Simpson to pack the survey camp from the base of one mountain to the next, setting it up in such a way as to ensure maximum comfort for the surveyors. Simpson was also to help carry the heavy survey equipment up the mountains. Over the course of the season, the Bow River trail enabled the survey crew to access 57 camera stations and take 305 views from various peaks.[42] Meanwhile, Simpson made his first two recorded mountaineering ascents.[43]

Arthur O. Wheeler (1860–1945)

Arthur Oliver Wheeler was born on the Wheeler family estate near Kilkenny, Ireland, on May 1, 1860. The aristocratic Wheelers, originally from England, had lived in Kilkenny for many generations. However, the 1876 economic depression forced them to sell their two prized estates and move to Collingwood, Ontario, where Arthur's father, Captain Edward Oliver Wheeler, took up the lowly post of harbour master.

Having obtained an education in Dublin and London, young Wheeler was able to apprentice as a land surveyor. He qualified as a Dominion Land Surveyor (DLS) in 1882 and devoted his entire career to the profession. He began his work in Ontario but soon moved west. He served as a lieutenant in the DLS Intelligence Corps during the Northwest Rebellion of 1885, and then he returned to the mountains, where he learned a new surveying technique: photo-topographic surveying, which required photographing the mountainous terrain from the tops of mountains. The Canadian government published the reports and maps from his surveys in the Selkirks in a book called *The Selkirk Range.*

While climbing in the Selkirks in 1902, Wheeler unabashedly named a peak he had climbed Mount Wheeler. His interest in naming peaks was given free reign when he was working for the Boundary Commission. In a decision many came to regret, the Geographic Board of Canada granted Wheeler permission to name the peaks in the Kananaskis area. He sought out namesakes amidst war generals, French villages, songs of the era and battleships – totally ignoring the first principle of alpine nomenclature: to reflect the natural history of the area. In a 1961 publication, R.M. Patterson commented that "the Rockies must surely be the worst named range in the world.... you can find there, enthroned in stone, a collaborator, a traitor to his country, sundry generals of dubious merit, and a demagogue... – to cite only a few of these ill-named mountains."[44]

Perhaps a more respectable legacy for Wheeler lies in his work with the Alpine Club of Canada. Early in the twentieth century, mountaineering clubs were being formed around the world. Having developed a lifelong interest in climbing through his work in photo-topographic surveying, Wheeler was interested in forming a Canadian club. Unable to generate much interest in an all-Canadian group, however, he eventually proposed forming a Canadian branch of the Alpine Club of America. When the idea came to the attention of Winnipeg-based nationalist and firebrand newspaper reporter Elizabeth Parker, she accused Wheeler of being un-Canadian in even considering forming a branch of an American club.[45] Together the two were able to generate sufficient interest in forming the Alpine Club of Canada (ACC). The inaugural meeting was held in Winnipeg in March 1906, with Parker and Wheeler generally considered co-founders.

In the club's early days, Wheeler directed its activities and organized its summer climbing camps. He served as president from 1906 until 1910, managing director from 1910 until 1926 and editor of the *Canadian Alpine Journal* from 1906 to 1927. He was elected honorary president in 1926 and continued in that office until his death. He was also elected to honorary membership in the Alpine Club (England) in 1912.

Throughout his tenure with the ACC, Wheeler was known as a vain and arrogant man with a strong will and volatile temperament. The reputation he had developed in survey camps for possessing a demanding nature and being subject to bouts of bad temper persisted. Perhaps his biggest drawback was his inability to treat subordinates with any measure of dignity or respect. They considered him to be abusive, conceited and autocratic; one surveyor who worked for Wheeler for years was prompted to comment that "he hated to see the return of the chief" to camp.[46] The following exchange between Wheeler and Fred Stephens, a well-known outfitter, which took place at the mouth of the Miette River, near Jasper, further illustrates Wheeler's difficult disposition, as well as the opinion of those he worked with. Wheeler: "Stephens, I always heard that you were a damn good man but you're not." Stephens: "Wheeler, I always heard that you were a s.o.b., and you are."[47]

Arthur Wheeler married Clara Macoun, daughter of botanist John Macoun (see page 54 for a brief biography), on June 6, 1888. As the Macouns were not of an aristocratic family, none of the Wheelers attended the wedding. Arthur and Clara had one son, Edward. The year following Clara's 1923 death, Wheeler married long-time close friend Emmeline Savatard. Arthur Wheeler died on March 20, 1945, at the age of 84.

Surveyor, mountaineer and author Arthur Wheeler is best known as the co-founder of the Alpine Club of Canada. This famous stance is known as the "he who must be obeyed" pose.

Clients of Note

In order to offer the most authentic wilderness experience, early outfitters typically consulted with one another to ensure that their parties would not meet up. Nevertheless, some meetings did take place, either on the trail or in camping spots. One such meeting took place in 1907. Jimmy Simpson was en route from Laggan to the Wilcox Pass area, escorting an unusual customer up the Bow–Mistaya–North Saskatchewan river corridor. The British Museum had commissioned Mrs. Mary de la Beach-Nichol, a 60-year-old Welsh adventurer, to search the Canadian Rockies for butterflies and moths. Having taken up Lepidoptera after raising six children, the "Butterfly Lady's" substantial means allowed her to develop a collection that was in the same class as those of such renowned collectors as the Rothschilds.

Outfitters in the early days were men of many talents. In this photograph, Jimmy Simpson is catching butterflies for renowned collector Mary de la Beach-Nichol.

De la Beach-Nichol and Simpson were near the base of Wilcox Pass when they met up with another adventuresome lady, Mary Schäffer.[48] "It was a comical meeting there of the two of us," Schäffer wrote, "one from the civilisation of London, one from Philadelphia. Shorn of every rag of vanity, the aristocratic little English lady rode out to meet me on her calico pony, clad in an old weather-beaten black gown, over her shoulder a 'bug-net', yet every inch a lady, from her storm-swept old Panama hat to her scarred and battered hobnailed shoes."[49]

Mary Schäffer had begun taking overnight trips through the mountains in 1904.[50] Two years later, she found a soul mate in New York geology teacher Mollie Adams. At the end of the summer, Billy Warren and Sid Unwin guided them over Pipestone Pass to the Kootenay Plains and north to the Columbia Icefield and Wilcox Pass.[51] They returned to the Kootenay Plains via Sunset Pass and the Cline River then continued on to the railroad by following the well-used trail along the North Saskatchewan River west to the Mistaya, south over Bow Pass and along the Bow to Laggan.

The next spring, Schäffer and her companions were back on the trail. She reported the trail from Laggan to Bow Summit to be in very poor condition:

> The fearful storms of the winter of 1906 and '07 had strewn the trail with timber, so that between jumping logs, chopping those we could not jump, and ploughing through the most disheartening muskeg, we at last, at nightfall, threw off the packs on a knoll with muskeg everywhere. Our first campfire was built in mud, we ate in mud, slept in mud, and our horses stalked around in mud, nibbling the few spears of grass which the late cold spring had permitted to sprout.... It did seem a rather dreary breaking-in for a whole summer's camping trip....[52]

They spent two nights with Beach-Nichol and Simpson in the vicinity of Mount Wilcox and the parties even enjoyed a meal together. Schäffer found that "it was such a treat to hear what some one besides ourselves had been doing, even though it was not from the outside world, and we talked far into the night around the camp-fire."[53]

Schäffer, Adams, Warren and Unwin returned to the area the following summer, this time accompanied by botanist Stewardson Brown, and packer and cook Reggie Holmes. They left Laggan on June 8 with 22 horses, repeating the beginning of their 1907 trip. The early start proved to be problematic. "From Laggan to the [North] Saskatchewan River via Bow pass, the weather and conditions under foot never for a moment permitted us to forget that the season was late and we were early," Schäffer explained. "Muskegs were at their worst and the ground sloughy without much intermission."[54]

Mary Schäffer and guide Billy Warren (shown here), together with Mollie Adams and packer Sid Unwin, travelled widely in the Rocky Mountains in the first decade of the twentieth century. Schäffer and Warren later married.

They travelled as far north as the North Saskatchewan River, where the party divided into three groups. Warren and Brown went to collect plants on the Kootenay Plains, Unwin and Holmes explored Glacier Lake, and the two ladies stayed in camp to do laundry "while the critics' backs were turned.... Long experience had taught us how to wash our hands in a teaspoon and take a bath in a tea-cup, so the blankets were manipulated with comparative ease in a hand-basin."[55] A few days later, the reunited party proceeded to Camp Parker, near the base of Mount Athabasca (just north and east of today's "Big Bend" in the highway). They stayed two days then turned east over Nigel Pass toward the Brazeau River.

Simpson found himself back in the Wilcox Pass area with another fascinating customer in the summer of 1910. The previous fall, intrigued by a painting of Dall sheep reproduced in an outdoor magazine, he wrote to the artist and invited him to come to the Rockies and paint Rocky Mountain bighorn sheep.[56] Carl Rungius obliged; in August 1910 Simpson found himself, and packer and cook Ernie Brearley, taking the famous painter along the Bow River to Bow Pass then down the Mistaya into Simpson's trap-line territory. Rungius sketched as he went. They continued to the North Saskatchewan, crossed the river and continued toward its source in the Saskatchewan Glacier. There they turned east and proceeded toward the top of Wilcox Pass, which offered views north toward the Arctic drainage and south toward the Athabasca Glacier, part of the massive Columbia Icefield. They went no farther, returning home along the same route.

Left: Old tree markers are still visible in Camp Parker, though the area is no longer used as a campground.

Opposite above: This trail marker, made in 1934, was photographed near Camp Parker in 2008. The arrow directs travellers toward the highway. Below is "NPC," presumably the National Parks Commission. The writing is still clearly visible and will likely last many more years.

Opposite below: Wildlife artist Carl Rungius first came to the Canadian Rockies at the invitation of outfitter Jimmy Simpson and ended up residing in Banff for part of each year thereafter.

Justin James McCarthy (Jimmy) Simpson (1877–1972)

The last and one of the greatest of the pioneer outfitters, Jimmy Simpson, was unique in many ways, but it was primarily his love of the arts that distinguished him from his fellow outfitters and guides. His fondness for music and books led to the accumulation of a major library, and his art collection was second to none in the Rockies, with many works acquired as a result of having guided the painters into the backcountry. He also collected stamps, gradually concentrating on Canadian imperfects and international air mails. Later in life, Simpson took up writing and painting, publishing mainly in outdoor magazines and selling his paintings to customers of his outfitting and lodge businesses.

Born on August 8, 1877, in Stamford, England, the rather rascally lad was raised by an aunt, due to the premature death of his mother. Although he attempted several trades during his youth, he was most successful at poaching on a nearby estate. By the time he reached 19, Simpson's family had run out of patience with him; they made arrangements for him to begin a farming career near Winnipeg. He left England in 1896, never to return.

Young Simpson recognized that he was cut out for a life in the outdoors, but he soon found that farming did not suit him. After relinquishing his money to the city taverns, he pawned his gold watch and chain to buy a train ticket to Calgary. He attempted to proceed to Golden as a stowaway but was thrown off at Castle Junction. He walked on to Laggan, where he encountered Bill Peyto, a fellow Englishman who profoundly influenced the course of his life.

Simpson worked a short stint for the CPR then began wandering, first west to Vancouver, and then south to San Francisco and on down the coast. He travelled through New Mexico before heading back along the West Coast. His travels led him to Rogers

Pass, where he signed back on with the CPR for the summer. He headed south again in the fall, but by May he had had enough of drifting. No doubt remembering the beautiful mountain scenery and his new friend Bill Peyto, he landed in Banff in the spring of 1898. He was offered a job by Tom Wilson and decided to stay.

Thus began a very distinguished outfitting career. First, however, young Simpson had to learn the tools of the trade. Bill Peyto and Tom Lusk had no trouble training him in the basics of riding a horse, packing and throwing the diamond hitch. The other necessity, being able to cook, he was already proficient at. The first task Wilson set for his new employee was to clear the trail to Bow Lake. Simpson fell in love with the area and prophetically declared that he would live there one day.

But first he had a career to establish. Simpson's first outing on the trail was not so much a trail ride as a responsibility to look after a group of wealthy Philadelphia Quakers, including the Vaux and Schäffer families, who had set up camp at Emerald Lake. It was enough for Simpson to decide that trail life suited him. Later, he learned how to handle guns and became one of the foremost big-game guides in Canada.

Aided by an inheritance from an English relative that he claimed not to know, Simpson began building up a string of horses and a collection of outfitting equipment so that he might establish his own business. By 1903 he had built a cabin and corrals in Banff, and that same year he did some outfitting for the Topographic Survey. The 1906 inauguration of the Alpine Club of Canada gave him additional work and led to many useful contacts.

He spent winters trapping and prospecting in the upper Bow Valley, where he enjoyed months alone in the wilderness. He was very proficient on snowshoes – a necessity for a trapper – and earned the name Nashan-esen, "wolverine-go-quickly," from the Stoneys because of his speed. By 1910 he had begun spending winters in town, where he enjoyed curling and playing and coaching hockey.

In 1913 the 36-year-old bachelor was smitten by Billie, a young Scottish lass who had immigrated to Canada and was working in the West. After three years of determined effort, he managed to convince her that life with a confirmed mountain man would not be so bad; they were married on January 31, 1916. They settled in Banff, where they raised two daughters and a son and became very involved in community life.

By 1921 Simpson was ready to pursue his dream of building a lodge at Bow Lake. He obtained a 21-year lease on a parcel of land and began construction in 1923. By the time the road was completed in 1940, the Simpsons had enlarged the lodge, named Num-Ti-Jah (Stoney for pine martin), and largely turned the operation over to their son. Their first season of winter operation was in 1962–63.

Jimmy Simpson died in the Banff Mineral Springs Hospital on October 30, 1972. Before his death, Simpson arranged to preserve most of his valuable art collection – including one of his own paintings – by selling it to Calgary's Glenbow Institute. Two years later, Parks Canada honoured him by holding a ceremony at Bow Lake and naming the mountain northwest of his Bow Lake lodge Mount Jimmy Simpson.

Jimmy Simpson came to Canada at age 19 and established himself as a guide, outfitter, hunter, builder and lover of the arts.

Later Journeys

By 1911 mountaineers were beginning to renew their interest in the peaks along the Bow Valley corridor. That year, the Alpine Club of Canada held its annual camp in the Consolation Valley, near Lake Louise. After the camp, a group of 11 attendees and ten horses took part in a six-day expedition up the Bow Valley. The three ladies in the group – including long-time mountain visitor Mary Vaux – rode, as did one gentleman and the two packers. The others, including ACC president Arthur Wheeler, walked. They left the horses at Bow Lake and crossed the Bow Glacier on foot. At the mouth of the Yoho Glacier, a packer met them with another group of horses. They proceeded to the ACC hut in the Little Yoho Valley, where others were waiting.[57]

The following year, the Warden Service had 30 miles (48 kilometres) of trail built from Laggan to Bow Summit. On August 6, 1913, mountaineer J.W.A. Hickson, Swiss guide Edward Feuz and outfitter and guide Ernest Brearley left Laggan intent on climbing some of the monumental peaks west of the Howse River.[58] They travelled easily up the Bow, camping at Hector Lake the first night and at Bow Lake the second.

By contrast, the trail down the Mistaya "was in an atrocious state."[59] Heavy rains earlier in the year had made a mess of the trail, which was strewn with fallen trees. It was extremely difficult to get the pack horses through. Beyond Waterfowl Lakes, down the Mistaya River to the North Saskatchewan "[t]he trail was poor and horribly wet, and fallen timber again proved trying to [the adventurers'] tempers."[60] They turned west at the North Saskatchewan River and set up camp on Freshfield Flats, near the base of Howse Pass.[61] They proceeded across the pass and back to Field along the route pioneered by Peyto and Collie.[62]

Ten years later, Hickson and Feuz repeated the trip, accompanied by climber Aime Geoffrion. The outfit was guided by Bill Potts with two helpers to look after the climbers' needs. On August 8, they were camped at Cinema Lake on Thompson Pass (near the Castleguard Meadows).[63] They returned by the same route along the Bow.

Canadian J.W.A. Hickson was a prolific mountaineer who claimed more than 30 first ascents during his career.

In 1916 John Wilson led his sisters, Bess and Slats (Dora), and his future wife, Jen, along the Bow River to the North Saskatchewan and east to the Kootenay Plains to visit his father's old homestead. Banff pioneer outfitter Tom Wilson had begun spending his winters running a combination horse ranch and trading post on the Kootenay Plains in the fall of 1902. The life seemed to suit him until he nearly died snowshoeing home for the Christmas of 1908.[64] Shortly thereafter, he sold the ranch to a partnership between his son, John, and Jimmy Simpson.

John Wilson and his companions left Lake Louise on August 10, 1916. They spent the night near Hector Lake then continued on past Bow Lake and down the Mistaya valley, where the perpetually rough trail required a lot of chopping. Approaching the North Saskatchewan River, the siblings were able to view Mount Wilson, named in their father's honour. They took a side trip to Glacier Lake, arriving on the Kootenay Plains ranch after a long ride on August 16. Bess later commented that "[t]he shacks looked mighty good to us"[65] and that a highlight of their stay was seeing the "shack where Dad spent his first winter at Kootenay Plains."[66] They found it a "very pretty spot but awfully lonesome."[67] After a spell of cold wet weather, they set out for home on August 21. Following their father's habitual route over Pipestone Pass, they arrived in Lake Louise on August 23.

Shortly thereafter, Jimmy Simpson, cook Watty Failes and wrangler Bob Alexander met up with their customers Robert Frothingham and George Martin in Lake Louise. The party headed north on August 26 with 14 horses and supplies for a one-month hunting trip. The first night's camp was at the favourite spot on Hector Lake, the second on Bow Lake. They continued down the Mistaya and up the North Saskatchewan to Nigel Pass, near the tongue of the Saskatchewan Glacier. They then turned east toward Cataract Pass and set up a base camp on Cataract Creek, where they hunted for the remainder of the month.[68]

Scientists were also busy in the area. Over the course of his career, geologist and palaeontologist Charles Walcott studied geology and collected fossils in nearly every part of the Rockies.[69] His first travels along the Bow–Mistaya–North Saskatchewan corridor took place in the summer of

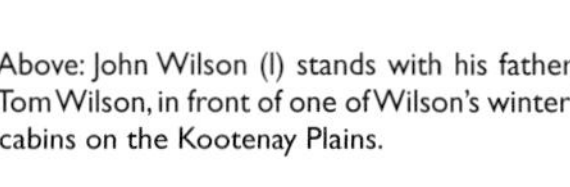

Above: John Wilson (l) stands with his father, Tom Wilson, in front of one of Wilson's winter cabins on the Kootenay Plains.

Right: (l–r) Bess Wilson, Jen (who later married John Wilson), and Dora Wilson in Banff in 1916. They accompanied John Wilson to the Kootenay Plains to see the old ranch where their father used to live during the winter.

1918. He, his wife, Mary Vaux Walcott, and camp manager Arthur Brown met packer Alex Mitten and their string of horses in Banff on July 6. After spending two days getting their outfit organized at Banff's Buffalo Park, they headed up the Bow Valley toward Lake Louise. They continued on to the favourite north end of Bow Lake, where they had set up a base camp by July 17. This was everyone's favourite camping spot in the area because of the view, flat land for tents, good water supply and fabulous scenery. They spent two weeks carrying out their studies from this camp, with Mitten proving himself to be far more than just a skilled packer; he was invaluable as a collector and geologic field assistant. After about two weeks, they moved on to the North Saskatchewan River and Glacier Lake. By August 28, they had returned down the Bow Valley and set up camp in the Vermilion Pass area.

It was about this time that the phenomenon of the guided tour began to take root in the Rockies. Unlike those who comprised the earlier parties that travelled the mountains, participants on these excursions had been recruited by advertising and often did not know one another prior to their alpine adventures. Caroline Hinman's Off the Beaten Track tours are a prime example of the organized guided tour.[70] In 1919 Jimmy Simpson outfitted her group to travel up the Bow Valley from Laggan to Nigel Pass. In 1925 she used the Bow Valley route to return from a long summer of travel in the Rockies, joining the North Saskatchewan from the Alexandra River.

Caroline Hinman was not the only one conducting guided tours in the 1920s. In 1923 Jasper's Jack Brewster initiated his Glacier Trail Tours, which took customers along Old Klyne's Trail from Jasper to the headwaters of the Brazeau River then over Nigel Pass to Camp Parker below Sunwapta Pass. From there the tours took a side trip to the Castleguard Meadows then reversed the Laggan–Sunwapta Pass route along the North Saskatchewan, Sunwapta and Bow rivers.

One such trip left Jasper on July 3, 1927.[71] With the assistance of horse wranglers Dorrel Shovar and Felix Plante, and cook Carl Madsen, Jack Brewster led Mr. and Mrs. S.C. Edmonds of Philadelphia, Otto and George Schultz of Chicago and Joan Robson of Jasper south over Maligne Pass. The adventurers, with their nine saddle horses and ten pack horses,

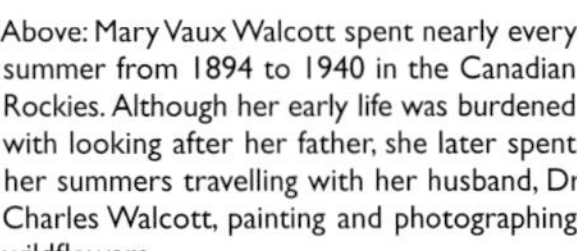

Above: Mary Vaux Walcott spent nearly every summer from 1894 to 1940 in the Canadian Rockies. Although her early life was burdened with looking after her father, she later spent her summers travelling with her husband, Dr. Charles Walcott, painting and photographing wildflowers.

Right: Caroline Hinman made a career of escorting teenaged girls on outfitted trips through the Canadian Rockies. Jim Boyce was her preferred guide, and Hinman went to great lengths to see that his hired men were kept away from her young charges.

arrived at the mouth of the Howse River on July 18. They took a side trip to Glacier Lake the next day then followed the Sunwapta River to a campground on the Waterfowl Lakes.

"We continued up the Mistaya River to its head at Bow Pass," Robson explained, "and crossed the pass which at that time of year was, from a botanist's point of view, at its very best. The flowers were simply beautiful."[72] They spent the night of July 21 camped at Bow Lake, which Robson declared would "remain one of [her] favourite lakes in spite of the fact that the mosquitoes led [them] a merry life, and it was impossible to move away from the smudge in comfort, and equally uncomfortable to stand by the smudge and breathe in smoke."[73]

The party proceeded down the Bow River to one final campsite before their arrival in Lake Louise. Though the scenery could not rival their previous night's abode, it was a camp none would forget: the party awoke in the morning to discover that all 19 horses had fled! Eventually the wayward animals were found and the campers proceeded on their way. Robson reported that by "mid-afternoon we were at Lake Louise Junction, and we scrubbed up and had dinner at Lake Louise Chalet. This marked the end of our trail trip, but not of its many pleasant memories."[74] Unfortunately, the tour business itself was also soon to be confined to the realm of memory; Brewster's enterprise was devastated by the Great Depression that began in 1929.

In the same year that Jack Brewster initiated his Glacier Trail Tours, Jimmy Simpson was finally ready to "build his shack" on the north shore of Bow Lake. The lumber and other building materials for what was to become Num-Ti-Jah Lodge arrived at Lake Louise by rail. Simpson cut the lumber to six-foot (1.8-metre) lengths then loaded it onto pack horses. Packing the horses was tricky, he admitted, but then again, "packing almost anything up the notorious 24 mile piece of the Bow Valley trail north of Lake Louise, ... was a battle."[75]

As construction proceeded throughout the 1920s, climbers continued to use the Bow Pass route to reach the popular Castleguard Meadows and

Jasper outfitter Jack Brewster started his Glacier Tours from Jasper to Lake Louise in 1923 but was hard hit by the Depression in 1929.

visit the Howse Pass area. Mountaineer J. Monroe Thorington travelled the Bow Pass route to the Castleguard Meadows in 1923. Three years later he returned to the Bow Valley, this time headed for the Howse Pass region.[76] He and fellow climber Max Strumia hired Jimmy Simpson and three helpers to guide their outfit of 21 horses. Swiss guide Edward Feuz rounded out the party, which left Lake Louise on June 30, reached the Howse River two days later and returned to Lake Louise on July 19 after a few weeks of successful climbing.[77]

In spite of chronic trail problems, the route's popularity was soaring. At the end of the following June, Jimmy Simpson took a pack train of 20 horses to the Howse Pass region with Harvard students Dyson Duncan and Twining Lynes and their Swiss guide, Ernest Feuz. Immediately upon returning to Lake Louise, he set out again toward the Castleguard Meadows with climbers Alfred Castle, his son Alfred, J.H. Barnes and Swiss guide Rudolph Aemmer.[78] At times, the trail up the Bow Valley must have seemed very busy indeed!

The last climber of note to use the Bow River trail was British politician, adventurer and mountain climber Leopold Amery. Determined to climb the peak named after him, Amery engaged Banff outfitter Jim Brewster to arrange an expedition. They set out from Lake Louise on August 15, 1929, and reached the North Saskatchewan three days later. At that point, they departed from this corridor, travelling up the Alexandra toward Mount Amery, which its 59-year-old namesake succeeded in climbing.[79]

J. Monroe Thorington (r) with climbing guide Conrad Kain on top of Trapper Peak in 1933.

Leopold Charles Maurice Stennett Amery (1873–1955)

Leopold Amery was born in Gorakhpur, India, on November 22, 1873, to an English father, Charles Amery, and a Hungarian Jewish mother, Elizabeth Leitner Amery. Amery's mother had immigrated to England after the 1848 revolution and converted to Christianity. Amery carefully concealed the fact that he had Jewish ancestry throughout his life, and this fact was only brought to light in a research paper published by William Rubinstein in the year 2000.[80] Amery was educated at Harrow School, after which he went up to Balliol College, Oxford, where he obtained a First in Classics in 1896 and was elected a fellow of All Souls College. A brilliant student, he was able to converse in eight languages other than English. In 1910 Amery married Florence Greenwood of Whitby, Ontario, with whom he had two sons.

His working life began with a year as a private secretary to politician L.H. Courtney, followed by ten years as a correspondent for the *Times*, during which he edited the seven-volume series, *The Times History of the South African War*. Amery was first elected to the House of Commons in 1911 and his political career continued until he lost his seat in 1929. Throughout his life, Amery wrote many books, mostly on political questions, but in 1946 he published *In the Rain and the Sun*, a description of some of his travels in various parts of the world, including the Rocky Mountains. Just before he died, he completed and published a three-volume autobiography, *My Political Life* (Volumes I and II, 1953; Volume III, 1955).

Amery enjoyed an active outdoor life and was especially noted for his mountaineering, which he pursued in various parts of the world until he was well into his 60s. He first came to the Canadian Rockies in 1909 and returned again in 1929 after his defeat in the election of that year. He had a special motive for returning that year as the Geographical Board of Canada had named a mountain in his honour in 1927. Amery was a member of the Alpine Club and served as its president from 1943 to 1945. He died in London on September 16, 1955.

World traveller Leopold Amery (r) managed to climb the mountain that was named in his honour. He is shown here on the summit with Swiss guide Edward Feuz Jr.

Alpine travel slowed considerably during the Great Depression of the 1930s. Still, people were getting married, and one young couple embarked upon an ambitious honeymoon trip by horseback from Calgary to Bella Coola on the Pacific Coast (see Route I above) in early July 1933. After a visit with the bride's parents, Cliff and Ruth Kopas led their five-horse pack train up the Bow River from Lake Louise on the newly built road pointing toward Jasper.

> We saw the road deteriorate from good gravel to dirt to a wagon road and finally to a muddy pack-trail. Mount Temple sank behind us, Mount Hector lifted in rocky eminence on our right and hard over on the left, Hector Lake caught the late afternoon sun. Evening and a swampy pasture for the horses coincided and we stopped for the night.... The next morning everything was crackling white with frost and we wasted no time breaking camp. That afternoon the bottle-green claw of Crowfoot Glacier holding a mountain in its clasp showed as we went around Bow Peak. Then the azure waters of Bow Lake smiled at us.[81]

They stopped at Bow Lake to spend some time at Num-Ti-Jah. They found "Jim Simpson, veteran of more than 30 years of trail making, trail riding and dude wrangling, ... voluble and entertaining" and very much enjoyed their visit with him, his family and alpinist J. Monroe Thorington and his wife.[82]

After three days at Bow Lake, the Kopases took a side trip to the Castleguard Meadows then headed east to Brazeau Lake, thus avoiding the difficult trip down the Sunwapta from Wilcox Pass (see Route III below).[83]

THE HIGHWAY

In 1931 the road between Banff and Jasper had been initiated as a Depression make-work project. Completed in 1939, it was officially opened as the Banff–Jasper Highway in 1940. In 1941, when Dr. Albert Wiebrecht and his family and friends from Milwaukee and Chicago hired mountain guides Edward Feuz and Ken Jones to guide them on a mountaineering trip near Howse Pass, Ralph Rink transported the large pack train from Banff to Lake Louise by train. He then trailed the horses to Saskatchewan Crossing on the newly completed gravel road. Meanwhile, the Wiebrecht party travelled by bus to meet the pack train at Saskatchewan Crossing. An easy one-day trail ride took them the rest of the way to Freshfield Canyon, where they set themselves up in a well-used campsite.[84] The days of struggling through muskeg along the base of Mount Hector had been consigned to history.[85]

When the road was improved and paved in 1961, its name was changed to the Icefields Parkway. The highway follows approximately the same route as the former trail, except that it is built higher on the side of the mountain to avoid the muskeg. Stutfield and Collie had suggested this change back in 1902, explaining that "where the trail descends to the level of the Bow River, the improvement ceases, and the muskeg and bog holes are now worse than ever ... the trail should be carried along the hillside past the base of Mount Hector, where, if once properly cut out, it could easily be maintained in a state of tolerable repair."[86]

Ken Jones (l) with Elizabeth Rummel, heading for Skoki Lodge in 1945. Jones was the first licensed Canadian mountain guide, and in his spare time, he helped his friends run backcountry lodges. Skoki Lodge was built in the early 1930s as a ski lodge.

The Trail Today

The old Native pony trail from Laggan into the North Country has entirely disappeared – some of it covered by the Icefields Parkway (which runs parallel to the Bow River as far as Bow Summit) and other parts (closer to the river and the muskeg) simply reclaimed by nature. Today's Icefields Parkway is one of Canada's most scenic highways by any measure. Despite the two high passes (Bow and Sunwapta) between Lake Louise and the Columbia Icefield, it is a favourite mountain route for bicyclists. Tourists in motorized vehicles ranging from motorcycles to giant diesel-powered motor homes travel the route by the thousands each summer. I hitchhiked on the road from Banff to Jasper while it was under reconstruction in 1961 and still fondly remember it by its former name, the Banff–Jasper Highway.

Less than two kilometres west of Lake Louise, the Icefields Parkway splits off to the right of the Trans-Canada Highway and begins its slow steady climb to Bow Summit. Most of the road was built on the side of Mount Hector to avoid the soft ground that caused such torment to early outfitters and their pack trains. The first campground is at Mosquito Creek; shortly thereafter you pass a viewpoint of the impressive Crowfoot Glacier. The mountains on both sides of the road provide a dramatic feast for the senses.

Bow Lake and its spectacular surroundings draw travellers on to Bow Summit. From there, the view down into the Mistaya valley is breathtaking. Even from an automobile, it is clear why the steep slope proved so difficult for horses. Proceeding steadily through the valley, you soon reach the camping area at Waterfowl Lakes and then the North Saskatchewan River at Saskatchewan Crossing. Even this close to its source the river is very fast and wide. There is no doubt about why the early outfitters had such difficulty fording it. From the crossing, the road begins climbing toward Sunwapta Pass and the Columbia Icefield. There are extensive gravel flats along the North Saskatchewan River and an impressive loop in the highway at the "Big Bend." Two campgrounds can be found between Saskatchewan

Crossing and the Icefields Centre, one at Rampart Creek and another at Wilcox Creek.

Even those travellers driving the Icefields Parkway in a comfortable modern vehicle who take time to stop at viewpoints and find quiet spots from which to look out over the magnificent river valleys will understand J. Monroe Thorington, who wrote:

> At last there was nothing to do but go; and go we did, into that wondrous land of far-off valleys where the great rivers of a Continent come leaping down in little brooks and arching waterfalls from the ice-tongues; where rise, beyond

The Icefields Parkway taken from the top of the "Big Bend," looking southeast along the North Saskatchewan River. This is only a fragment of the dramatic scenery offered to motorists, bicyclists and hitchhikers along the highway.

the old horizon, the castellated crags and snowy spires we had read and dreamed of. It was the valley of the Bow and the trails of the Waputik that led us onward to unvisited corners of the northern ranges. We were not pioneers ourselves, but we journeyed over old trails that were new to us, and with hearts open. Who shall distinguish?[87]

Above: Crowfoot Glacier originally had more of the "toes" that led to its naming. By the time this photo was taken in 2008, over a century's worth of glacial recession had left only two toes.

Opposite: This early morning photo of the Lower Waterfowl Lake was taken from the campground on the south end of the lake. Ducks and loons could still be seen swimming in the lake, just as they did a century ago.

Trail Guide

Lake Louise to Sunwapta Pass (Columbia Icefield)

Maps 82 N/8 Lake Louise
82 N/9 Hector Lake
82 N/10 Blaeberry River
82 N/15 Mistaya Lake
83 C/3 Columbia Icefield
Gem Trek Bow Lake and Saskatchewan Crossing
Gem Trek Columbia Icefield

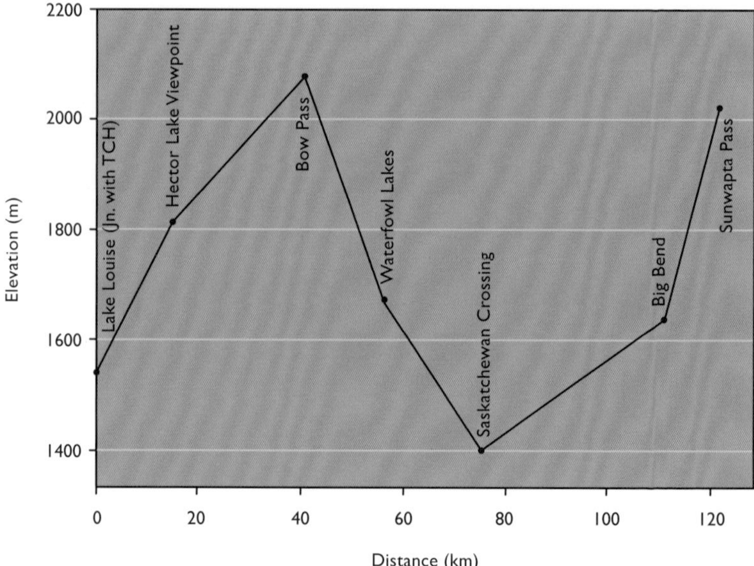

Trailhead

The entire Lake Louise to Sunwapta Pass trail is now a road. The road starts in Lake Louise village and follows the Trans-Canada Highway west for less that 2 km. It then splits off to the right on the Icefields Parkway and follows it north to Sunwapta Pass and the Columbia Icefield. A description of the route is given in the Trail Today section, above on page 134.

The Pipestone Pass route to the North Saskatchewan River, which was reputed to have fewer muskegs than the Bow River route, passed through the Pipestone Valley (centre of photo). Neither the river nor the trail is readily apparent here.

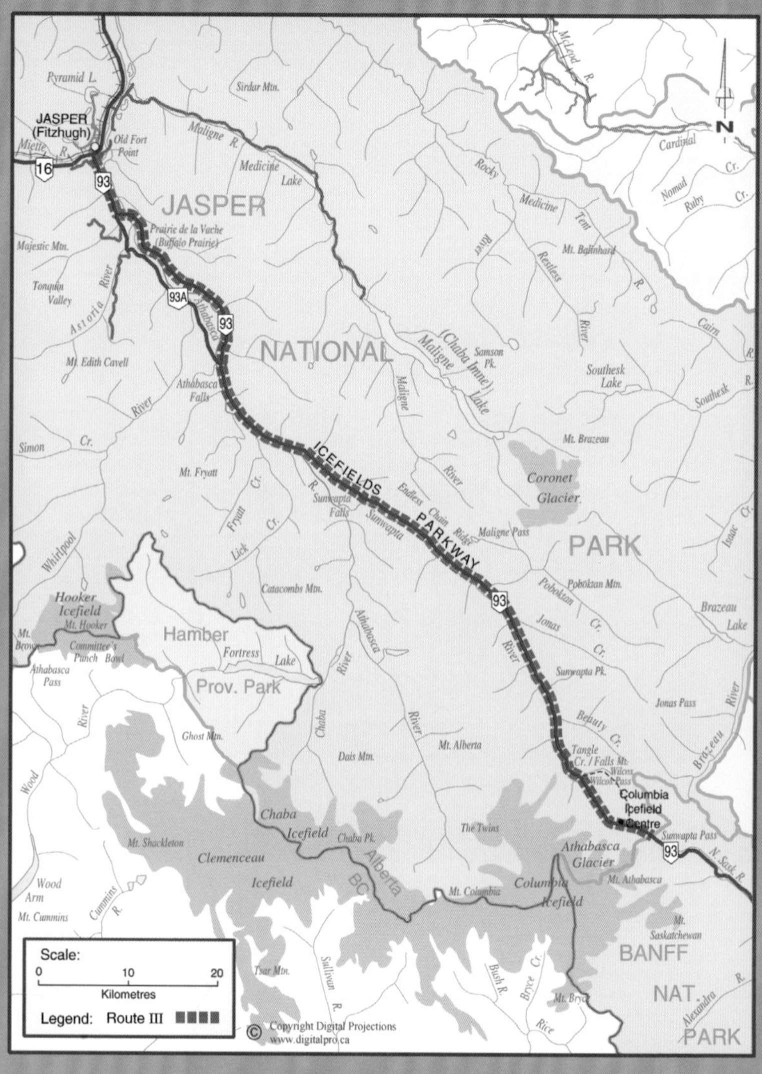

The historic trail from Sunwapta Pass (Columbia Icefield) to Fitzhugh (Jasper).

Route III

Glaciers, Canyons and Waterfalls: Sunwapta Pass to Fitzhugh (Jasper)

The final quarter of the twentieth century saw an entirely new use of the old pony trail between Banff and Jasper. For one weekend each spring today's highway became the site of the Jasper to Banff Relay. Race stations were set up at approximately 17-kilometre intervals along the route, and the road filled up with cars, trucks, buses and motor homes carrying runners to their start stations and escorting them while they ran. This 24-hour race through spectacular mountain scenery gained such world-wide popularity that the organizers and Parks Canada had to limit the number of entries. Toward the end of the century, the race had run its course and was terminated for a variety of reasons – though not for lack of interest on the part of runners.

Both Janice and I participated in the race in 1987, me as a runner and Janice as a young spectator. This was a memorable race for me. I had just purchased my first car with electric locks. It was very early in the morning when I arrived at the designated station to begin my leg of the race. I left family and friends in the car while I checked on the progress of my team member. For some unknown reason, I left the keys in the ignition of the car. After I departed, the other adults and Janice decided to follow me to the check point. This meant that my younger daughter, Susan, was alone in the car. Unhappy with this situation, she decided to leave, too. Knowing that the last one out of the car should lock the doors, she made good use of the new electric door locks by opening a rear door, reaching through to the driver's side and pushing the lock. A resounding clunk assured her that she had successfully executed the task. She closed her rear door and headed down the road to join the others. The keys, of course, were still in the ignition!

Nothing could be done until I had run my leg of the race. I found a ride back to the car. Since getting a locksmith on the Icefields Parkway very early on a Sunday morning did not seem likely, I borrowed a hammer and pounded on the car's smallest window until it broke. Anyone who has ever had to take a hammer to their new pride and joy will know how I felt. The deed accomplished and the window taped up, we continued down the parkway, somewhat less jubilant than we had been several hours earlier.

The author first ran the Jasper to Banff Relay in 1983. Each of 17 runners ran a 16- to 17-kilometre section to complete the 24-hour relay in the scheduled time.

Chronology

1893 Arthur Coleman, professor of geology at the University of Toronto, and his brother, Lucius, proceed north from Lucius's Morley ranch on the Bow River east of Old Bow Fort overland to the Sunwapta River and along the Athabasca to the mouth of the Miette.

1896 Walter Wilcox and fellow American R.L. Barrett set out north along the Bow and North Saskatchewan rivers. Finding the route blocked by the Athabasca Glacier, they take the next valley to the east and cross the pass known today as Wilcox Pass into the Sunwapta valley. This is the first recorded crossing from the drainage of the North Saskatchewan River to that of the Athabasca over the pass (Wilcox Pass) that most travellers will use until the Banff–Jasper Highway is built in the 1930s.

1898 Bill Peyto guides J. Norman Collie and companions Hugh Stutfield and Herman Woolley north to the Columbia Icefield. Collie and Woolley climb Athabasca Peak, becoming the first non-Aboriginal men to see the tremendous expanse of the Columbia Icefield. They cross Wilcox Pass and climb in the Sunwapta valley before returning along the Bow to Laggan.

1901 Dan Campbell guides mountaineer Jean Habel north over Wilcox Pass. They spend a week camped at Fortress Lake before returning to Laggan.

1904 Jim Brewster and friends make the first trip between today's towns of Banff and Jasper. They spend two months camped at their destination: the confluence of the Miette and Athabasca rivers.

1907 Billy Warren and Sid Unwin guide Mary Schäffer and Mollie Adams up the Bow River into the Athabasca River drainage and along the upper reaches of the Athabasca to Fortress Lake.

Asked to make the inaugural climb of the Alpine Club of Canada, the Coleman brothers attempt Mount Robson. They travel the Pipestone Pass route to the North Saskatchewan then on to the Athabasca and Miette rivers, eventually arriving at the mouth of the Robson River. They are unsuccessful in their climb.

1908 Mary Schäffer and Mollie Adams retrace portions of their 1907 trip then turn east to rediscover Maligne Lake. They then retreat to the Sunwapta and proceed north, going as far as Tête Jaune Cache.

1909 Stanley Washburn reaches the Yellowhead Pass after several attempts (see pages 101-104). Outfitted by Fred Stephens, he and his party reach the Banff–Jasper trail by travelling along the Brazeau River and over Nigel Pass. They cross Wilcox Pass then proceed to the Miette and their destination.

1910 The Otto brothers spend 21 days on the Banff–Jasper trail, moving their outfitting business from Field to Jasper.

Jasper outfitter Curly Phillips takes photographer Byron Harmon, climber Reverend George Kinney and Swiss guide Conrad Kain to the railway in Laggan, follows Mary Schäffer's route over Maligne Pass then joins the Banff–Jasper route where Poboktan Creek empties into the Sunwapta River. Phillips convinces Kain to accompany him on the return trip, and they complete the round trip in less that one month.

1912 Jasper's Jack Brewster takes a pack train along the same route used by Curly Phillips in 1910.

1917 Arthur O. Wheeler, president of the Alpine Club of Canada, follows the entire route of today's Icefields Parkway and declares that the route will become world renowned.

1924 Byron Harmon, famed Banff mountain photographer, and his friend Lewis Freeman, a freelance writer and adventurer, make the only major trip from Lake Louise to Jasper during the 1920s.

The party leaves Lake Louise on August 16 on a 70-day, five-hundred-mile (805-kilometre) pack-train trip to Jasper.

1925 Renowned Japanese mountaineer Yuko Maki and a six-man party, as well as Swiss guides Heinrich Fuhrer and Hans Kohler, and amateur Swiss climber Jean Weber, make the first ascent of Mount Alberta, astonishing the North American climbing community.

1927 A.J. Ostheimer and two fellow Harvard students, John de Laittre and Rupert Maclaurin, plan a nine-week climbing expedition from Jasper, outfitted by Curly Phillips. They travel south along the Athabasca as far as the Sunwapta, where they turn west.

Tangle Falls, at the junction of the north end of the Wilcox Pass trail and the Icefields Parkway, is a scenic stopping spot today.

This pencil drawing of botanist David Douglas was executed by his niece, Miss Atkinson. Douglas crossed Athabasca Pass in 1827 and started a controversy that took mountaineers 66 years to solve.

History

Tempted by Giants

With fur traders and railway surveyors focused on east–west transportation, few travellers continued past the Columbia Icefield along the Sunwapta and Athabasca rivers until the early mountaineers of the fourth period of exploration were enticed by the challenges of more northerly peaks. The first recorded trip north of Sunwapta Pass along the Laggan–Jasper trail was inspired by a desire to solve the "David Douglas controversy."

David Douglas was a botanist who had travelled west with the 1826 fur brigades. On his return the following spring, he crossed Athabasca Pass en route to Jasper and the east. At the top of the pass, he paused to climb a mountain to the north, which he named Mount Brown and declared to be 16–17,000 feet (4877–5182 metres) high. This estimate ranked the mountain as the highest known peak in North America. To the south, Douglas identified another peak of similar height, which he named Mount Hooker. His "tall" tales were an enticement mountaineers could not resist.

Arthur Coleman, professor of geology at the University of Toronto, and his brother, Lucius, had been trying to reach Athabasca Pass for several years, approaching from both the Columbia and Athabasca rivers.[1] The Coleman brothers did not use outfitters: when they first travelled in the eastern Rockies in 1892, they hired Stoneys to guide them through their traditional hunting grounds between the Red Deer and North Saskatchewan rivers. On subsequent journeys, they took only a local farmer or rancher as a helper. Their horses either came from Lucius's ranch or were purchased from neighbouring Stoneys.

The Colemans' 1893 attempt began at Lucius's ranch in Morley, east of Old Bow Fort on the Bow River. The party consisted of the two brothers, their friend, Professor L.G. Stewart, and Frank Sibbald, a young rancher from the Morley area. As Coleman later explained, "Sibbald was hardy and resourceful, as Western ranchers are apt to be, was thoroughly familiar with horses, and a fair camp cook, so that he served our purpose admirably, though he had seen little of the mountains, and did not profess to be a climber."[2] Growing up in Morley, Sibbald had also learned both the Cree and Stoney languages, which proved useful in gaining information from the Natives they met along the trail.

After the usual hassles of breaking in new pack horses and trying to pack others for the first time that season, the party set out from Lucius's ranch on the afternoon of July 8, 1893. Arthur Coleman was careful to point out that although they had had the good luck of securing an efficient man like Sibbald, expediency called for all to share in the necessary work of packing, camping and cooking.

Professor, geologist, explorer and mountaineer A.P. Coleman set out to locate and climb Mount Brown, thus resolving the "David Douglas controversy."

That summer's packing was particularly challenging, as the party had decided that carrying a canvas boat would spare them the hassle of building rafts to cross the larger rivers. They found that:

> It proved to be very useful, but most inconvenient to pack on a pony, since it measured four and a half feet when done up in its canvas cover. It was always catching in trees or getting out of balance on the pack, and cost ponies and packers an immense amount of hard feeling and strenuous language, so that more than once we resolved to leave it behind, though we always relented.[3]

The first part of their journey was relatively straightforward, as they were able to follow a well-established Stoney trail through the foothills to the Red Deer River and north to the Kootenay Plains. From the plains, they followed the Cline River west to Cataract Creek. The creek led them north to Jonas Pass, the source of Jonas Creek. They followed the creek across the Endless Chain Ridge, entering the Sunwapta valley north of Sunwapta Pass.

It is here that their journey connected with the Laggan–Jasper trail – or rather, with what was to become the northern stretch of the Laggan–Jasper trail; they were the first party to record travelling the northern portion of this route. They began by setting up camp on the Sunwapta so the horses could rest for a day while the men explored the Sunwapta valley. The day's adventures included climbing a 10,000-foot

A bighorn sheep enters the Sunwapta River on the gravel flats near the Icefields Parkway. Bighorn sheep were not only the favourite wild meat of early travellers but were also often hunted to procure a trophy set of horns.

(3048-metre) peak just east of the Sunwapta's headwaters, which gave them a marvellous view of the terrain ahead.

Nevertheless, they found the following day's journey down the Sunwapta extremely difficult. The path (probably a game trail) was strewn with fallen timber. Coleman explains:

> The three axes were got out and we took turns at chopping a way through the miles of windfalls, sometimes following an old trail, but oftener losing it. The work was disgustingly slow, and once we forded, in despair of making our way on the east side, but a few miles down forded back again. Our rate of travel dropped to five or six miles a day instead of the usual fifteen or twenty.[4]

They breathed a sigh of relief upon reaching the mouth of Poboktan Creek. The remainder of the route to the Athabasca was familiar to them; they had travelled it the previous year on their way to discovering Fortress Lake.

They had not, however, travelled north of the Athabasca. Once again, they delved into challenging new territory as they forged what would become the pony trail to the fur-trade post of Jasper House (east of the future railway town of Fitzhugh, which later became the town of Jasper). Their objective was the gateway to the fur traders' Athabasca Pass: the mouth of the Whirlpool River, which flowed into the Athabasca from the west. The adventurers struggled through the burnt woods, finding that their "axes were getting very dull from striking stones in slashing out the trail, and no work with the file and whetstone would give them a serviceable edge, so that the constant chopping grew very hard, though we took turns in the attack."[5]

As they neared the Whirlpool's latitude, Stewart measured the sun's angle with his sextant daily, but by August 6 they "were almost in despair."[6] The burnt timber was so thick that it was nine o'clock before they emerged "out of the woods into open ground with a little pasture."[7] They had been on the trail nearly a month, and their destination continued to

The old fur-trading post of Jasper House, located along the Athabasca River east of the town of Jasper. This is how it appeared to Charles Horetzky, a member of Sandford Fleming's survey team, on January 15, 1872.

prove elusive. "Days like this," Coleman lamented, "made one wish he had never come out in search of high mountains."[8] Fortunately, he went on, "after this, things improved and we could sometimes trot over bits of prairie covered with long grass or through groves of unburnt timber.... The trail became well beaten and well blazed, and we wondered by whom the work had been done."[9]

They were beginning to think they might have missed the Whirlpool River when a wide valley opened to the west. They crossed the river to find a very recently travelled trail leading up the valley. They began to suspect that they had reached the Miette River, which led to Yellowhead Pass. They travelled far enough to determine that the valley ran west, not south as the Whirlpool did. Concluding that the river was indeed the Miette, and that they were in the vicinity of present-day Jasper, they turned their horses eastward the next morning, recrossed the Athabasca and headed back south.

They set up camp about eight miles (13 kilometres) up the valley then proceeded to walk along the riverbank, keeping a careful watch for the Whirlpool. Coleman reports:

> Before long Stewart noticed that the water on the other side was greener than on ours, and, reaching a bend in the Athabasca, we saw the real Whirlpool, with its narrow valley reaching far to the south into the mountains. In our hurry to cut a way through the timber and hustle up the unwilling ponies, we had passed the mouth of the river, coming in on the opposite shore of the Athabasca without noticing it, and had paid the penalty with fifty miles of travel and four days' loss of time.[10]

The fact that their determined search had resulted in the first known trail from the Sunwapta River to Jasper along the Athabasca would have been little consolation.

But the confidence that they were now on the right track bolstered the men's spirits enough that they immediately set about ferrying their goods across the Athabasca for the third time. The remainder of their trip to Athabasca Pass was both successful and disappointing; the final outcome was that they discovered the heights of Mounts Hooker and Brown to be substantially less than recorded by Douglas.[11]

Nevertheless, the Coleman brothers were not the only adventurers interested in discovering the long-unused fur-trade route over Athabasca Pass and the supposed giants Hooker and Brown. Walter Wilcox's 1892 explorations north of Laggan had taken him as far as Bow Pass (see Route II above). But he had not been able to find any information about the region north of the pass, and trails appeared to be non-existent.

The combined appeal of unexplored country and the mystery of Hooker and Brown were sufficient to entice Wilcox back to the region. He and fellow American R.L. Barrett set out from Laggan in the summer of 1896. Tom Wilson provided their outfit, assigning American Tom Lusk as head guide with the assistance of Fred Stephens as packer and Arthur Arnold as cook. He supplied enough food for 60 days, with ten pack horses to carry the outfit and five saddle horses for the men.

The trip was uneventful until the party reached the North Saskatchewan River (today's Saskatchewan Crossing). At that point, they were unsure about whether it was the Alexandra River (north of the Crossing, and flowing from the west) or the more northerly branch (the North Saskatchewan) that would lead them to the Athabasca. As mountaineers often did when faced with such a decision, they climbed a mountain to gain perspective. The Alexandra valley appeared to be blocked by a glacier, so they continued up the North Saskatchewan – in spite of the misgivings provoked by the depth of its canyons.

Having crossed today's Sunwapta Pass, they found what would become the route of the Icefields Parkway blocked by the Athabasca Glacier. (It receded considerably in the ensuing century.) They took the next valley to the east, crossed the pass known today as Wilcox Pass and entered the Sunwapta valley. This is the first recorded crossing from the drainage of the North Saskatchewan River to that of the Athabasca River over Wilcox Pass – a route widely used until the Banff–Jasper Highway was built in the 1930s.

Once in the Sunwapta valley, Wilcox's group found Coleman's blazed trail and followed it, hoping that it might lead to the Committee's Punch Bowl on top of Athabasca Pass. Instead, they found themselves at Fortress Lake. It had taken them 44 days to reach and explore the region, leaving 14 days' worth of food for the return trip. Rationed to two light meals a day, they managed to successfully attain their destination.

British mountaineer J. Norman Collie was also intrigued by the Hooker–Brown controversy. Although the Coleman party had already discredited the supposed giants, their allure was not easily diminished. When climbing Mount Freshfield (in the Howse Pass region) in 1897, Collie had seen a tall mountain to the north and wondered if it might be Mount

The Athabasca Glacier, Icefields Parkway and the Icefields Centre taken from the trail to Wilcox Pass. This photo gives an indication of how far the glacier has receded since 1896, when it blocked passage through the valley.

Brown or Hooker. Back in Britain that winter, he spent his spare moments planning another trip to the country north of Laggan. Among his objectives were "to reach the actual sources of the vast river systems of the [North] Saskatchewan, the Athabasca, and the Columbia; to explore and map out the unknown mountain country where they take their rise; to locate, and perhaps to climb, the semi-fabulous peaks of that region; [and] to rehabilitate, if the facts permitted, the outraged majesty of Mount Brown."[12]

Collie and his companions, Hugh Stutfield and Herman Woolley, left Liverpool on July 14, 1898, aboard the steamer *Labrador*. By Friday the 29th they had arrived in Banff; the following Sunday they proceeded by train to Laggan, where outfitter Tom Wilson had arranged their outfit. Bill Peyto was to serve as head guide, assisted by packers Nigel Vavasour and Roy Douglas, and cook Bill Byers.[13] Thirteen horses carried the supplies and working men; the mountaineers were to walk. Mountaineers often preferred to walk, both because most were not experienced horsemen and because they needed to get into shape for climbing after a winter of inactivity at office jobs.

Collie's party left Laggan at noon on July 31 and spent the next nine days following the Pipestone Pass route to the confluence of the three forks of the North Saskatchewan River (today's Mistaya, Howse and North Saskatchewan rivers).[14] Realizing that the mountaineers would require horses to cross the rivers, they cached a considerable portion of their supplies to free up three pack horses. They managed to cross the Mistaya and the Howse without mishap but found the North Saskatchewan to be in flood.

In spite of the fact that Wilcox's trail was on the east side, Peyto advised against fording the river. Instead, the party tried to force its way up the west bank. "The next four days," Stutfield and Collie later recounted, "were one long battle with woods, muskegs, and rivers, the cussedness of pack-horses and our own tempers.... Had we had less resolute and hard-working men than Peyto and his staff, our trip must inevitably have resulted in failure."[15] In spite of almost ceaseless cutting from early morning until late afternoon, they only advanced three to four miles (five to six kilometres) a day. Making matters worse was the aggravation of seeing "across the river and within a stone's-throw of us, moderately open country with a good trail, and yet to be unable to get to it."[16]

On the fifth day, Peyto and Vavasour went ahead to search out a trail. They returned declaring the situation to be impossible. "Ignoring Peyto's picturesque language," Stutfield explained, "Collie remarked that the weather was exceedingly warm; they must be very thirsty; and that whiskey and water wasn't a bad drink when you couldn't get any better. To this they agreed. We waited."[17]

They soon acknowledged that unless they were prepared to give up on the journey, they would have to risk crossing the North Saskatchewan. Stutfield explained that Peyto, "after several plucky attempts ... forced his mare across, and the outfit followed. The water in mid-stream was almost up to the horses' backs and the current very swift; but the bottom was good, and we all got over with nothing worse than wet legs and damp packs."[18]

Having made their peace with the mighty North Saskatchewan, the party followed it to Sunwapta Pass. They crossed the pass to camp near the Athabasca Glacier (which they named, along with Athabasca Peak). Climbing the latter, Collie and Woolley gained the distinction of being the first non-Aboriginal people to view the tremendous expanse of the Columbia Icefield, the centre of the greatest accumulation of ice in the Rocky Mountains. In the meantime, Peyto, Stutfield and Vavasour proceeded to Wilcox Pass in search of game to supplement the party's dwindling food supply.

On August 24, the entire party crossed Wilcox Pass and set up camp in the Sunwapta valley. Collie named the pass after Wilcox, the first person recorded to have crossed it. He also named an adjacent peak for Wilcox. Though the group did not proceed any farther along the Laggan–Jasper trail, they did spend some time climbing in the Sunwapta valley. Low food supplies pushed them back across the pass to their cache on the Mistaya River. They then followed the Bow River route to Laggan, climbing a few peaks along the way. Their backcountry journey concluded in Laggan on September 10, and although they did not reach their main objective, they did enjoy a successful summer of climbing.

The twentieth century dawned with the advent of another important trip of discovery, that of Germany's Professor Jean Habel.[19] Habel had been to the Rockies before; his 1897 attempt to climb Mount Balfour from the west resulted in a new route through the Yoho Valley.[20] Four years later, having heard the story of Collie's high mountain off to the north, he set out for Athabasca Pass with the ambitious goal of exploring the area between the Wood River, which flows west from Fortress Lake, and the more southerly Bush River.

Unlike most early mountaineers, Habel chose to travel with only his guides for company. Tom Wilson outfitted him for his 1901 journey, providing Dan Campbell as guide, Joe Barker as packer and Fred Ballard as cook. They left Laggan on July 2 with 12 horses. Though Habel published an account of his trip in the journal, *Appalachia*, he devoted little of it to describing life on the trail.[21] We do know, however, that he and his guides crossed Wilcox Pass in good weather on July 15 and set up camp at Fortress Lake on July 22, where

Professor Jean Habel explored extensively in the areas around Yoho Valley and Fortress Lake during his two summers in the Rockies.

they remained until July 28. His lofty ambitions had evolved into an exploration of the area around Coleman's Fortress Lake.

Habel was a taskmaster. His men did not enjoy his company and were particularly irritated by what they saw as his superior attitude. He and Ballard had particular difficulty getting along.[22] While exploring in the Fortress Lake area, Habel was constantly frustrated in his attempts find the blazes the Coleman party had left on trees, many of which had been destroyed or blurred by forest fires. On hearing of Habel's sudden death shortly after his return to Europe, the unsympathetic Ballard muttered, "Good, he can see the blazes now."[23]

Nevertheless, Habel did carry out the first recorded exploration around the north side of Mount Columbia near the headwaters of the Athabasca River. As was common on such early exploration trips, the party ran short of food and had to leave sooner than they would have wished. They left the Fortress Lake area on August 12, arriving back in Laggan on August 24, after spending eight weeks on the trail.

From Laggan to Fitzhugh

Though the Colemans had pioneered the route from Jonas Creek to Fitzhugh, Walter Wilcox had established a trail around the Athabasca Glacier (Wilcox Pass), and the Collie party had discovered the massive Columbia Icefield, until 1904 no one had travelled the entire route up the Bow Valley, across Bow Pass and Sunwapta Pass and on to Fitzhugh. This honour belongs to Banff's Jim Brewster and a party he guided. The party consisted of Detroit drug company executive Dr. Sterns and three Princeton classmates: Philip Moore, Fred Hussey and Halsey Williams. Brewster himself guided them, assisted by George Harrison, Fred Tabuteau and Bob Logan as packers and Sid Collins as cook. Their destination was the confluence of the Miette and Athabasca rivers (near present-day Jasper).[24]

They needed 18 horses to carry the supplies and provisions the men would require for the two months they planned to spend hunt-

Members of the first party to travel the entire distance from Banff to Jasper are (l–r standing): Bob Logan, Sid Collins, Phil Moore, George Harrison and Jim Brewster; and (l–r seated) Fred Tabuteau and Halsey Williams.

Mary Schäffer and Mollie Adams, the first non-Aboriginal women to venture far into the wilds of the Rocky Mountains, were not averse to bringing along some small comforts from civilization. They are shown here pumping up air mattresses.

ing and exploring in the area. Since a pack train of this size advances slowly, Bill Potts led the horses ahead and waited for the main party at Athabasca Falls. When the others caught up, the combined party continued down the Athabasca River and set up permanent camp at the mouth of the Miette. Over the course of the summer, several excursions were taken from this base camp, including a trip by Brewster and Hussey back to Banff. Near the end of September, outfitter Bill Brewster (Jim's brother) arrived with Bert Sibbald to help Bill Potts escort Dr. Sterns and his trophies back to Banff. The remainder of the party continued on to complete another historic trip (this one over Yellowhead Pass) before making their way back to the Columbia River and eventually to Banff via Field.

At the time, it was virtually unheard of for women to undertake such adventurous travel in the Canadian Rockies – though not for want of interest. As adventurers like the Princeton classmates; Habel; Stutfield, Collie and Woolley; Wilcox; and the Colemans shared stories of their exploits, two particular women listened more intently than most. At last, Mary Schäffer explained, "[o]ur cups splashed over. Then we looked into each other's eyes and said: 'Why not? We can starve as well as they; the muskeg will be no softer for us than for them; the ground will be no harder to sleep upon; the waters no deeper to swim, nor the bath colder if we fall in' – so – we planned a trip."[25]

One of the stated objectives of Mary Schäffer and Mollie Adams's first grand adventure was to travel up the Bow River, explore the sources of the North Saskatchewan River, cross into the Athabasca River drainage and follow the upper reaches of the Athabasca to Coleman's Fortress Lake. The two women, guide Billy Warren and packer Sid Unwin left Laggan on June 20, 1907, with 11 horses. They found the trail up the Bow strewn with timbers from the previous winter's unusually heavy storms, and the muskeg was worse than usual due to a wet spring. Nevertheless, Schäffer explains:

> From the summit of the Bow Pass ... we gazed to the north on as fair a picture as dreams could suggest. Winter was reluctantly loosening its hard grasp upon those open meadow-like slopes; the snow lilies..., the pale pink spring beauties..., and the bright yellow violets..., were flirting with the butterflies and bees, pretending to be utterly oblivious to the mountains of snow all about them. We thought, as we wended our way over the crest of the pass, of lovely Peyto Lake which lay but a few hundred yards to our left, but with new fields to conquer, there was no time for a glimpse of the older friend.[26]

Three days later, following a night at Upper Waterfowl Lake, they met Tom Wilson coming from the Kootenay Plains with a herd of about 60 horses, en route from their wintering range to their summer work-places in Banff and Laggan. This was where Schäffer met "the flower of the band, 'Nibs', who was to leave his chums and follow the vicissitudes of his mistress for the next four months. Just an Indian-bred pony, with a coat that only one who loved him could say was beautiful, he proved himself a perfect trail horse."[27]

Silencing their dread at the thought of having to ford the wide and powerful stream, Schäffer and her trail mates continued following the Mistaya toward the North Saskatchewan River. They crossed the Mistaya without incident at 3:30 then proceeded to the bigger challenge: a ford of the North Saskatchewan one mile (1.6 kilometres) to the west. Sid Unwin mounted the horse considered best able to handle himself in the rapidly flowing water – Nibs – and headed into the stream. As Schäffer later writes:

> He slowly waded in, the water would creep higher and higher about the plucky pony's shoulders till horse and rider

The original horse trail and Icefields Parkway both followed the shore of Lower Waterfowl Lake.

> almost disappeared from view; they would then back out and try it farther up or down, then emerge to a bar and work over the next channel in the same way. At last after fifteen minutes, we saw him a distant speck in the brilliant setting sun on the north shore. He waved his hand, and we knew that our yet untried horses could be got over without much danger of getting washed down-stream.… Yes, we got over without having to swim, but one never wants to take those large rivers which are fed by the great icefields, other than seriously.… The horse, his head facing up stream a little to avoid the full flow of the onrushing waters, bends his whole body to the force; the rider, to help him in the balance, leans in an opposite direction.… It is then that you think of your guide's words of caution: 'If your horse rolls over, get out of your saddle, cling to his mane, tail, or any thing you can get hold of, but don't let go of him altogether! He may get out, you never will, alone.'[28]

They continued past Mount Wilson up the "North Fork" to the base of Sunset Pass, where the Alexandra River flows into the North Saskatchewan from the west. Inspired by the substantial number of animal bones strewn around, they named the spot Graveyard Camp. They established a cache then proceeded north to the source of the North Saskatchewan, over Wilcox Pass and down the Sunwapta to its junction with the Athabasca. At that point, they left the Banff–Jasper trail to proceed south along the Athabasca to Fortress Lake.

Little did they know that the Coleman brothers, whose trip reports they had fruitlessly sought out, were about to return to the Athabasca region. The Alpine Club of Canada had been formed in 1906, and Mount Robson, Canada's highest known peak, had been chosen as a fitting inaugural climb for the fledgling club. ACC president A.O. Wheeler had asked the Coleman brothers – the best-known and perhaps only Canadian mountaineers and explorers of the day – to attempt the climb on behalf of the club.

Accepting the assignment, the Colemans had to decide which route would best lead them to their destination (near British Columbia's Fraser River, west of the Yellowhead Pass). They considered three options. They could have taken the train to the Columbia valley and followed the old fur-trade route over Athabasca Pass to the Athabasca River then west along the Miette River to Yellowhead Pass. But having attempted that route some 20 years earlier, the Colemans quickly eliminated it from the list of options. Travelling west from Edmonton would have constituted a second possible route, but hearing that the trail was both in poor condition and traversed many miles of boring foothills country, the Colemans chose the southern route.

In the 1890s, the Colemans had often begun their expeditions at Morley. In the intervening years, a number of factors – including the Stoneys' settling on a reserve and the transformation of their hunting grounds into national parks – meant the trails from Morley had fallen into disrepair.[29] Having been advised that there were fewer muskegs on

(l–r) Reverend George Kinney and Lucius Coleman on the main glacier, Mount Robson. Lucius Coleman travelled with his brother, A.P. Coleman, on most of his trips in the Rocky Mountains; his Morley ranch supplied the majority of the outfit.

the Pipestone Pass route to the North Saskatchewan, they decided to start at Laggan and follow this trail.[30]

They left Laggan on August 3, 1907. As usual, they had provided their own outfit, this time consisting of six pack horses and four saddle horses. Riding the latter were Arthur and Lucius Coleman; a third climbing partner, the Reverend George Kinney; and local rancher Jack Boker, who was to serve as packer. After six days of travel, they reached the North Saskatchewan River at the Kootenay Plains then followed the south bank of the river west to the Mistaya, forded it and proceeded north along the North Saskatchewan River.[31] They passed Mount Coleman and pushed on over Wilcox Pass to camp near the summit.

The next morning, to their great surprise, they discovered that the Schäffer party was camped nearby. Mary Schäffer later described the encounter:

> In my half dreams I heard a distant shout, and thinking it was one of the men calling for a helping hand to bring in the horses, paid no further attention. Imagine my surprise, on hearing a clearing of the throat at our very tent door, to wake fully and behold a strange, full-bearded, spectacled, and most respectably clad man [Lucius Coleman].... Bowing as though in a drawing-room and doffing his spotless hat, he said, 'I hope I don't intrude?' Not wishing to be outdone in politeness even under such limited circumstances, I struggled up as far as the confines of the sleeping-bag would permit, ducked as gracefully as possible, and murmured 'Certainly not.'[32]

Perhaps due to the onset of wintry weather, the Coleman party moved camp only a short distance later that day. It was August 17 and snowing heavily. Meanwhile, Schäffer's party was taking a Sabbath day of rest. Later in the day, having realized who their morning visitor was, Schäffer and Warren decided to take advantage of the opportunity to return a lost horse to their neighbours.

"It was a delightful surprise," Arthur Coleman wrote, "to have a charming woman ride in out of the snow in the midst of the Rockies and join us at our lunch of bannock, bacon, and tea."[33] Moreover, he went on, "we got some very useful hints for the future from our guests, for Warren is an experienced and resourceful man who knows most of the mountain trails that can be reached from Laggan."[34]

The next day dawned bright and clear and the snow melted quickly. As the loads were heavy and some of the horses were getting sore backs, the Colemans decided to cache their canvas boat and some 50 pounds (23 kilograms) of supplies before proceeding. As it turned out, they did not return by this route and never saw the items again.

Continuing along the Laggan–Jasper trail, they proceeded over Wilcox Pass to the Sunwapta River, which they followed to the mouth of Jonas Creek. From there on they found the trail to be just as they remembered from the previous trip: a jumble of fallen timber and rock slides interspersed with swamps and muskeg. Eventually they reached the main Athabasca valley, passed the Whirlpool River on August 28 and continued north to the mouth of the Miette, where their course turned westward toward the Yellowhead Pass.

Though Schäffer and her party, which consisted of Mary and Mollie Adams, with guide and packer Billy Warren and Sid Unwin, greatly enjoyed their summer on the trail – and handily accomplished their stated objective – they did not fare much better than the Colemans in fulfilling the true goal of their journey. Schäffer had heard rumblings of a hidden northern lake, *Chaba Imne,* known only to Aboriginal peoples, and longed to experience the serenity of its shores. She did not manage to locate it in 1907 but returned the following year, armed with a map drawn by Stoney Sampson Beaver, who as a child had accompanied a hunting party to the lake.

The map enabled Schäffer to fulfil her dream of reaching today's Maligne Lake – with enough summer left over to continue exploring northward. Hoping to avoid retracing their footsteps, Warren and Unwin attempted to chop a trail down the Maligne River to Fitzhugh. After several days of intense chopping, they were forced to concede to the density

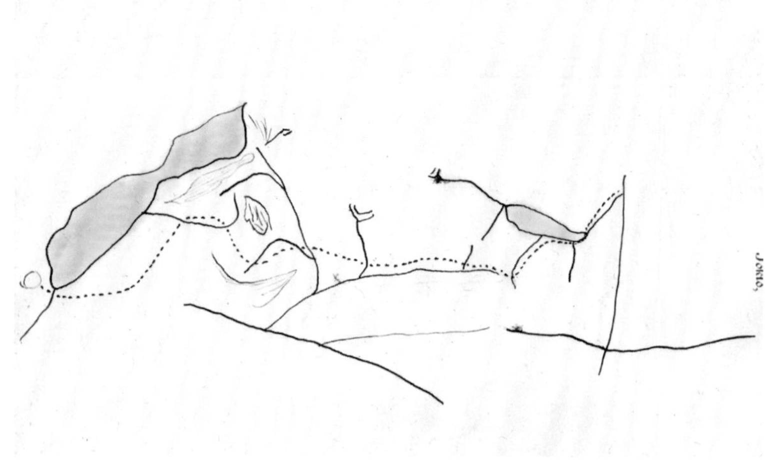

Mary Schäffer's second trip in search of *Chaba Imne* (Maligne Lake) was aided by a map drawn from memory by Sampson Beaver, who had visited the lake as a boy. Even with the map, Schaffer's party had some difficulty locating the lake.

of the fallen timber. They retreated all the way back to Poboktan Creek, which they followed through the Endless Chain Ridge to the Sunwapta River and the old pony trail between Laggan and Fitzhugh. The trail led them along the Sunwapta to its junction with the Athabasca River. This time, they continued following it northwest along the Athabasca to its junction with the Miette, the end of the Laggan–Jasper trail. A well-beaten trail along the Miette led them toward their new goals: Yellowhead Pass and Tête Jaune Cache.

Another determined adventurer retraced the latter portion of the Schäffer party's journey the very next year. The enthusiastic but naïve Stanley Washburn had first visited the mountains in 1897 (see page 101). He returned in 1901 and 1903, despite the fact that he seldom accomplished his travelling objectives. But in 1909 he finally fulfilled his dream of travelling overland from the foothills to the Yellowhead district and into central British Columbia. Having struggled with incompatible travelling companions in the past, he decided to travel with only his outfitter Fred

Stephens, Fred's brother, Nick, as packer, a cook named Tom, and a mining engineer called Sawyer who was to map the route. The party employed 22 horses to carry them and their gear on their four-month expedition.

Having begun their journey during June in the eastern foothills town of Lacombe, the adventurers entered the mountains along the North Saskatchewan River. They proceeded north to the Brazeau River, which they followed to its source near Nigel Pass. It was here that they gained access to the Banff–Jasper trail.

Finding the snow on top of Nigel Pass still deep from winter storms, Washburn explained that "with picks and shovels, we hewed out a kind of a way along a soft bit of cliff, and after an hour we took the horses up it, one at a time, feeling their way, with ears pricking forward and back every instant and short snorts of apprehension and dismay at the insecurity of their footing on the narrow ledge."[35]

Two days later, they reached the foot of Wilcox Pass, which they proceeded to cross without incident. They continued on down the Sunwapta, only to find the Athabasca in full flood due to a late spring melt. Reaching the Miette was not to be as straightforward as they had hoped. Washburn explains:

> As we pushed down the valley, the river would strike from one side to the other, making it necessary to cross and recross at least half a dozen times during a single drive, and each crossing brought on a problem to be solved on its own merits.... When the day's drive of six or eight hours had brought us to a camping place, everyone was wet, half frozen and disgusted, but, ... the troubles of the day are forgotten the moment unpacking commences. In ten minutes the tents have been put up, with front flaps thrown wide open and big fires burning within six feet of their yawning mouths, while the heat sends columns of steam from the saturated canvas. In half an hour more, all is as dry as in a house, and beds are laid under the canvas, books are dragged out of packs, and the balance of the day passes

> with the ease and comfort which, it often seems to me, no civilisation can ever quite equal.[36]

Eventually the Athabasca became too large to cross safely. As others had done before them, the weary travellers settled on a route down the east bank. After about two weeks, they found themselves opposite the mouth of the Miette. The party continued east along the Athabasca, halting five miles (eight kilometres) upstream from the Swift homestead. Lewis Swift had lived in the valley since 1893. Four years after arriving in the area, he married Suzette Chalifoux, and the two decided to raise their family there. Their home was a landmark; nearly everyone passing through stopped to visit and perhaps to purchase fresh vegetables, milk, eggs or some beautifully handcrafted clothing from the Swifts.

The Washburn party built a raft to ferry themselves and their supplies to the north bank of the Athabasca. They swam the horses across the river then continued to the Swifts' place to reorganize the outfit. Any horses and equipment deemed unnecessary for the trip across the Yellowhead Pass and down the Fraser were left in the Swifts' care. Then, after a period of rest, Washburn's party continued on, finally enabling him to cross the Yellowhead Pass and visit Tête Jaune Cache.

Members of the 1911 ACC–Smithsonian expedition (l–r) James Shand-Harvey, Reverend George Kinney, Conrad Kain and Curly Phillips resting in camp before the latter three set out for Laggan. The remaining members of the party are (l–r) Charles Walcott Jr., Harry Blagden, Ned Hollister, J.H. Riley and Arthur Wheeler.

The Wonder Trail

When A.O. Wheeler, president of the Alpine Club of Canada, first travelled the Banff–Jasper pony trail, he predicted that "through dense primeval forests, muskeg, burnt and fallen timber and along rough and steeply sloping hillsides, a constant flow of travel will demand a broad well-ballasted motor road.... This wonder trail will be world renowned."[37]

Although he did forecast correctly, Wheeler's constant flow of traffic was still but a mere trickle in 1910. Early in the season, the Otto brothers had spent 21 days moving their outfitting business from Field to Jasper along the trail. That fall, well-known Jasper outfitter Curly Phillips led the

first party through the mountains "from steel to steel" – from the Grand Trunk Pacific Railway at Fitzhugh (now Jasper) to the Canadian Pacific Railway at Laggan (now Lake Louise).[38]

Having completed some survey work in the Maligne Lake area, Wheeler asked Phillips to take his companions – photographer Byron Harmon, climber Reverend George Kinney and Swiss guide Conrad Kain – to the railway in Laggan. They followed Mary Schäffer's route over Maligne Pass, joining the Banff–Jasper route where Poboktan Creek empties into the Sunwapta River. They continued over Wilcox Pass and Bow Pass to follow a good trail down the Bow to Laggan. The entire journey was accomplished in a mere 12 days. After briefly resting the horses, Phillips proceeded to retrace the route before the passes were completely blocked by snow. He managed to convince Conrad Kain to accompany him; they reached Fitzhugh in 13 days. Never before had such a short round trip between Laggan and Fitzhugh been attempted. Phillips accomplished the feat in less than a month.

Two years later, Jack Brewster added to the trickle of "wonder trail" travellers by guiding a pack train along Phillips's route. One of his guests was Mary Jobe, a woman who would earn a reputation in the mountains for her travels north of the Athabasca River. Wheeler himself made the trip along the "wonder trail" in 1917, following the entire route of today's Icefields Parkway. The trip took ten days.[39]

Nevertheless, trips along the route remained infrequent during the 1920s. Perhaps the reason was best summed up by the most experienced of the old-time outfitters, Jimmy Simpson: "Frankly, the country is so damn big that the Jasper region those days seemed to be 'the outer rim of the back of beyond,' that weeks were needed to get there & with only cayuses to do it on it seemed a fantasy."[40]

Of course, the remoteness of the region was bound to attract some adventurers. Caroline Hinman's Off the Beaten Track tours used small portions of the Banff–Jasper route in the 1920s.[41] The occasional mountaineering group also recorded a trip. In 1922 Allen Carpe and friends travelled along the Athabasca River from Jasper to Fortress Lake to climb;[42] the following year the Appalachian Mountain Club used the Wilcox Pass–Sunwapta–Athabasca River route on their way to Jasper and Mount Robson.[43]

Byron Harmon (1876–1942)

About the same time as the Kodak Company came out with its first roll film in the late 1880s, a young man in Tacoma, Washington, decided that since he could not afford the Kodak version, he would build himself a pin-hole camera. In spite of his rather crude equipment, the young man must have had some success with his images. Byron Harmon went on to become world famous as a photographer of mountain scenery.

Born on February 9, 1876, Harmon was the last of three children. His father deserted the family shortly thereafter, leaving Harmon's mother, Clara Smith Harmon, alone with the children. Harmon was a sickly child, suffering from typhoid and asthma, the latter of which afflicted him his entire life.

Pursuing his love of photography, which had consumed him since childhood, Harmon opened his first portrait studio in Tacoma in the mid-1890s. But his keen spirit of adventure did not allow him to remain there long. By the end of the decade, he had packed up his equipment to become a travelling photographer. Ultimately, his travels took him to Banff. He stayed only briefly at the time but returned early in the twentieth century to begin his life's work: photographing every major peak in the Rockies and Selkirks.

Though Harmon had begun with portraiture, his main interest was mountain landscape photography. As a result of his early hiking, riding and climbing trips through the Rockies, he was soon able to advertise the largest collection of postcards in the Rockies – over one hundred images. Postcards were held in very high esteem at the time, and sales formed a large part of his business. Movies were also an important part of his life; a moving picture camera often accompanied him on his travels.

Byron Harmon was a renowned Banff photographer who set himself the task of photographing most of the major peaks in the Canadian Rockies.

When the Alpine Club of Canada was formed in 1906, Harmon became its official photographer. Cherishing the exposure the club's early climbing camps gave him to guides, outfitters, mountaineers, explorers, scientists and surveyors, Harmon attended most. He was regarded as a hardy companion on the trail, a man of boundless energy who was always willing to help out, be it chopping trail or rounding up the horses. In one 24-hour period, he hiked 36 miles (58 kilometres) with a full pack – a task few would tackle.

His involvement with the ACC paid rich dividends. The *Canadian Alpine Journal* published many of his images and ACC connections led to invitations to join the extended journeys that enabled him to fulfil his dreams of photographing major peaks. In 1911 he participated in a major expedition to the Purcells and, in 1912, a three-month trip from Lake Louise to Mount Robson. He later became a founding member of both the Trail Riders of the Canadian Rockies and the Skyline Trail Hikers of the Canadian Rockies.

Although the organized trips allowed Harmon to obtain many fine photos, the group agenda sometimes restricted his ability to capture the images he wanted. Eventually he began organizing his own expeditions. His last major adventure in the Rockies was his 1924, 70-day, five-hundred-mile (805-kilometre) trip from Lake Louise to Jasper with Lewis Freeman, a writer who documented the trip.

As well as being an ardent traveller, Harmon was also an entrepreneur. He set up his Banff studio in 1908, followed by a moving picture theatre in 1912. He extended his business interests to a number of other shops, and his participation on local committees, boards and associations led to his esteem as a model citizen.

In 1920 Harmon's international reputation took a giant leap forward with the invitation to serve as a representative to the International Congress on Alpinism in Monaco. As part of the congress, he showed movies of the Canadian Rockies and set up a display of 150 mountain prints. The trip was an outstanding success, leading to invitations to exhibit in Europe in 1923–24. Harmon continued to travel frequently in the following years, including a trip around the world in 1930.

Harmon was married twice: to Maud Moore in either 1909 or 1910 and to Rebecca Pearl Shearer in 1928. He had three children from his first marriage: Aileen, Lloyd and Don. Few other details of his personal life are available. Harmon's final years were spent quietly in Banff, suffering from hypertension. He died on July 10, 1942, at the age of 66. His prints are still regularly displayed and sold in Banff, more than 60 years after his death.

But the only adventurers to undertake a major trip from Lake Louise to Jasper during the 1920s, were Banff's famed mountain photographer, Byron Harmon, and his writer friend, Lewis Freeman. The party left Lake Louise on August 16, 1924, on a 70-day, five-hundred-mile (805-kilometre) pack-train trip to Jasper. Head guide was Soapy Smith, assisted by wrangler Rob Baptie and cook Ulysses La Casse. Sixteen horses and two dogs rounded out the party. Freeman wrote that:

> Our only real frills were the radio and its satellites, the carrier pigeons and the typewriter. The radio was Freeman's idea, 'born of the memory of the real entertainment the Grand Canyon party had had from a similar outfit a year previously.' ... The carrier pigeons were Harmon's idea. He had been breeding homers at Banff for a year or two but had never had a chance to try them out in the mountains.[44]

Harmon and Freeman began their ambitious 1924 expedition by following the Bow River past Hector Lake to Bow Lake. They set up camp at the north end of Bow Lake on August 20. In spite of the late-summer snow drifting down from the sky, they were able to receive some radio stations and release several pigeons. The pigeons were never recovered, but someone did mail the messages they were carrying to Banff. The party broke camp the following day, crossing Bow Pass to the Mistaya valley. Unfortunately, a pack horse badly damaged the radio en route.

Finding the area east of the head of Upper Waterfowl Lake to be a good spot for photography, the party stayed a day before continuing down the west side of the lakes and on to the North Saskatchewan. They crossed without incident then camped three days while they waited for the weather to improve enough to get good movie footage of the horses fording the river. They set out again on August 26, travelling as far as the mouth of the Alexandra River. They spent the night at Schäffer's Graveyard Camp then left the Banff–Jasper trail for a side trip to the Castleguard Meadows.[45]

They returned to the Banff–Jasper trail by crossing the tongue of the Saskatchewan Glacier, proceeding downstream along the beginnings of the North Saskatchewan River to Nigel Creek and then turning north to cross Sunwapta Pass. They set up camp under the snout of the Athabasca Glacier (near today's Icefields Centre), where they spent four days resting the horses and photographing the glacier.

The final region Harmon wanted to photograph was the head of the Athabasca River at the base of Mount Columbia. The men led the pack train over Wilcox Pass on a very fine day. Early the next morning, they left their comfortable camp a mile below timberline to continue their journey toward the Sunwapta. They followed the river north then crossed to the east, where they picked up a well-defined trail to the Sunwapta Ranger Station. Two hundred yards below the ranger station they found a sign pointing to Fortress Lake and a solid log bridge across the Sunwapta. They continued past the lake to the source of the Athabasca, where Harmon photographed to his heart's delight.

Returning to the Banff–Jasper trail, the party camped at the mouth of the Chaba River, which drains Fortress Lake, and took a side trip to the lake. They left the lake on September 29, reaching Jasper on the afternoon of October 1. Their route followed the Athabasca fairly closely all the way, the last two days over a well-cut trail.

When Lewis Freeman and Byron Harmon travelled from Lake Louise to Jasper in 1924, they brought carrier pigeons along for the ride. Though the pigeons belonged to Harmon, Freeman is shown here releasing one.

More Lofty Ambitions

All but one of the trips discussed thus far originated in the south. This is not surprising given that most adventurers accessed the Rockies via the southerly Canadian Pacific Railway. Even after the Grand Trunk Pacific was completed through Fitzhugh (Jasper) in 1911, few travellers used the town as an access point to the south. But by the 1920s, some trips had begun originating in Jasper. One such adventure, which was quite remarkable from a mountaineering perspective, took place in the summer of 1925. Renowned Japanese mountaineer Yuko Maki had been reading *A Climber's Guide to the Rocky Mountains of Canada* by Howard Palmer and J. Monroe Thorington and was immediately inspired by the challenge presented on the cover: a photo of Mount Alberta with the caption: "A Formidable Unclimbed Peak of the Range." Maki assembled a six-man party, which arrived in Jasper on July 6. The group stayed at Canadian National Railway's Jasper Park Lodge and acquired the services of Canadian National's two professional Swiss guides, Heinrich Fuhrer and Hans Kohler. At the guides' request, Jean Weber, a visiting amateur climber from Switzerland, joined the party.

Under the guidance of Cliff Rollins, the entire party left Jasper on July 11 with 39 horses and five wranglers. They followed the Lake Louise–Jasper trail along the Athabasca until its junction with the Sunwapta, where they left the main trail and followed the Athabasca south, almost to its headwaters. They established camp at the junction with Habel Creek, southwest of their objective: the massive Mount Alberta. On July 22, they succeeded in climbing it. Astonished by the foreigners' marvellous feat, the North American climbing community essentially ignored it.[46]

Two years later, another amazing mountaineering adventure originated in Jasper, following the route of the Japanese expedition along the Athabasca. A.J. Ostheimer and two fellow Harvard students, John de Laittre and Rupert Maclaurin, had planned a nine-week climbing expedition. The title of their report was "Every Other Day," which referred to their military-like plan to climb a new mountain every second day.[47] Renowned Jasper outfitter Curly Phillips supplied the outfit: French Cree

The Japanese and Swiss alpinists who conquered Mount Alberta: (l–r) photographer Nagatane Okabe, geologist and geographer Masanobu Hatano, botanist and artist Yukio Mita, expedition doctor Tanezo Hayakawa, expedition secretary Seiichi Hashimoto, leader Yuko Maki, outfitter Fred Brewster, Jasper Park Lodge mountain guide Heinrich Fuhrer, Swiss amateur climber Jean Weber and Jasper Park Lodge mountain guide Hans Kohler.

Adam Joachim as packer, young Kennie Allen as packer's assistant and Don Hoover as cook. Hans Fuhrer served the team as Swiss guide, with amateur Swiss climber Jean Weber as assistant.

With 17 pack horses and eight saddle horses, the party left Jasper at 3:45 p.m. on June 22. They rode along the Athabasca River, crossed the Whirlpool and proceeded to Athabasca Falls, following the approximate route of today's Highway 93A. From the falls, they followed the bank of the Athabasca River as far as the mouth of the Sunwapta, where they left the Lake Louise–Jasper trail and proceeded south along the Athabasca River to accomplish one of the greatest ever mountaineering feats in the Canadian Rockies: scaling a total of 36 peaks in 63 days, 27 of them first ascents. Even more remarkable was the fact that Ostheimer personally scaled all but two of them.

Six years later, another remarkable adventure took place along this trail. A large pack train of 27 horses and ten people emerged from Poboktan Creek and headed north toward Jasper in July 1933. Cliff and Ruth Kopas were on a honeymoon trip from Calgary to Bella Coola on the Pacific Coast (see Routes I and II above). After emerging from a side trip to the Castleguard Meadows, they met up with a group of professional outfitters heading to the goldfields of the Cariboo: George Riviere, his wife Maggie; her sister, Annie Clark; and two men, Ray Cyrl and Slim Black. The two parties agreed to travel together as far as Jasper. They headed east to Brazeau Lake in order to avoid the difficult trip down the Sunwapta from Wilcox Pass. At the warden cabin on the Brazeau, they met up with Warden Charlie Matheson; his wife, Mona; and their ten-year-old guest, Ralph Wells.[48] As they were also heading to Jasper, the three parties agreed to travel together.

The combined groups crossed Poboktan Pass and met up with the Sunwapta trail at the mouth of Poboktan Creek, from which they proceeded north. After a short distance along the Sunwapta, they reached the Mathesons' home, where they spent a day resting the horses and three waiting out a rainstorm. They returned to the trail on the fifth day and soon met the crew that was building the road from Jasper to Lake Louise. Here the Mathesons traded their horses for a pick-up truck, crossed the Athabasca on the newly completed highway bridge and proceeded on to Jasper. The remainder of the group continued on the old pony trail down the east side of the river. They dropped down a steep pitch of trail near Old Fort Point and crossed the Athabasca on a substantial bridge to arrive in Jasper, where the remaining two parties split up.[49]

The Kopases took a side trip to the Tonquin Valley before proceeding westward. They arrived in the Bella Coola valley on October 10, after some very difficult travel, and viewed the ocean for the first time. Cliff wrote in his diary:

> We reached the sea five days ahead of schedule. Fifteen hundred miles. The Bella Coola valley is the most beautiful spot we have ever seen. It has never seen a depression. It has an

Park Warden Charlie Matheson at his Brazeau Lake Warden Cabin in the 1920s. Matheson later married Mona Harragin, one of the first two licensed female guides in Canada's national parks.

> air of contentment, like that of an old mountaineer smoking his carved pipe and watching the evening shadows rise out of the valley below. We will stay here.[50]

Unfortunately, the story does not have a happy ending. Only sixteen months after arriving in Bella Coola, Ruth died of complications during childbirth. Their son, Keith, was adopted by Ruth's sister and husband in Calgary. Cliff lived the rest of his life in Bella Coola; still, over the years he and Keith were able to develop a strong bond. That bond also extends to Keith's half-sister who lives in Bella Coola. Cliff died in Bella Coola in 1978.

Over the course of the next decade, Wheeler's "broad, well-ballasted motor road" wended its way through the river valleys of the North Country to Jasper. The original road was officially opened as the Banff–Jasper Highway in 1940 and was completely rebuilt in the early 1960s. The resulting modern mountain road was paved in 1961 and renamed the Icefields Parkway. The road, which remains essentially unchanged today, handles thousands of vehicles a day during the summer months. It is unlikely that either Thorington or Simpson could have anticipated the traffic load the original gravel road would eventually bear.

Cliff and Ruth Kopas travelled overland from Calgary to Bella Coola on the Pacific Coast, hitting many of the scenic spots in the Rockies along the way. Cliff is seen here after arriving in Bella Coola, and Ruth is en route on Dream, a gentle pack horse that became an ideal saddle horse.

The Trail Today

Shortly after crossing Sunwapta Pass on the Icefields Parkway, today's travellers arrive at the Icefields Centre. The landscape is dramatically different than it was a century ago, when ice blocked passage along what has now become the road. Even today, the tongue of the Athabasca Glacier is visible across the highway from the centre, and travellers can drive almost to its mouth.

The Athabasca Glacier is a small tongue of the massive Columbia Icefield, as are the Saskatchewan Glacier and others visible from the Icefields Parkway.[51] These tongues began receding at the end of the last mini ice age, sometime near the middle of the nineteenth century, and have receded considerably since then. Prior to 2008, tourists were allowed to experience walking on the ice within a roped-off section of the glacier located across from the Icefields Centre.

When Walter Wilcox arrived in the summer of 1896, he pioneered the route through the next valley to the east as a means of circumnavigating the glacier. Early travellers often commented on the herd of bighorn sheep on Wilcox Pass, which many used as a food source. Fortunately the travellers weren't numerous or hungry enough to prevent today's visitors hiking the popular Wilcox Pass trail from enjoying the sight of sheep in their natural setting. The trail, which can be hiked as a day hike, provides a good view back over the Sunwapta valley and the glaciers on its west side. (See trail guide below on page 184).

From the Icefields Centre, the highway drops rapidly along the Sunwapta River. Tangle Creek and Falls mark the northern end of Wilcox Pass. Beyond Beauty Creek, the valley bottom becomes quite level with wide gravel flats. The highway passes Jonas Creek, where the Coleman brothers exited the mountains before the easier Poboktan Creek route was discovered. Sunwapta Falls marks the beginning of the trail to Fortress Lake, near where the Sunwapta flows into the Athabasca. The river is wide and fast flowing at this point; the highway follows closely in many sections.

The next major point of interest is the powerful Athabasca Falls, where the original road crossed the river and continued on its west bank. The Icefields Parkway stays on the east side until near the Wabasso Lakes. The original pony trail continued on the east side the entire way to Jasper; today's trail from Old Fort Point (near Jasper) to Buffalo Prairie is likely close to where the original pony trail ran.

As with the southern portion of the Icefields Parkway, the section from Sunwapta Pass north to Jasper runs through spectacular mountain scenery with many viewpoints. There are campgrounds and hostels along the way and a major visitor centre at Sunwapta Falls, in addition to the previously mentioned Icefields Centre.

Moose are often seen along the Icefields Parkway in the Sunwapta Valley. This young bull in spring velvet, photographed from the highway, is attempting to rid himself of insects.

Trail Guide

Distances are adapted from existing trail guides: Patton and Robinson, Potter, and Beers, and from Gem-Trek maps. Distances intermediate from those given in the sources are estimated from topographical maps and from hiking times. All distances are in kilometres.

Sunwapta Pass to Jasper

Maps 83 C/3 Columbia Icefield
83 C/5 Fortress Lake
83 C/6 Sunwapta Peak
83 C/12 Athabasca Falls
83 C/13 Medicine Lake
83 D/16 Jasper
Gem Trek Columbia Icefield
Gem Trek Jasper and Maligne Lake

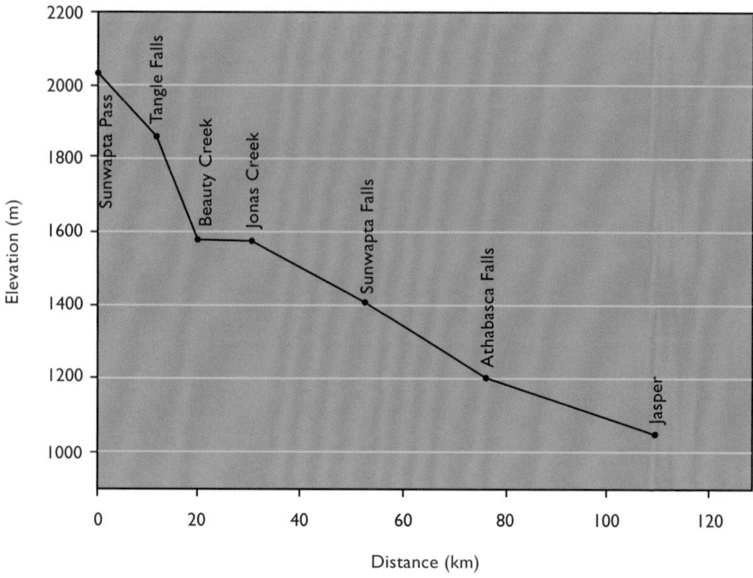

Trailhead

The Sunwapta Pass to Jasper route is a road today and begins on the Icefields Parkway at Sunwapta Pass, just south of the Columbia Icefield. See the Trail Today section on page 182 for a description of the route.

Mountain goats often descend from their lofty domain on Mount Kerkeslin to visit the natural mineral licks on the high banks above the Athabasca River, near Goat Viewpoint. They are most prevalent during the spring moult and were likely there in the early twentieth century when the Brewsters passed by.

Walter Wilcox's Route around the Athabasca Glacier (Wilcox Pass)

Maps 83 C/3 Columbia Icefield
83 C/6 Sunwapta Peak
Gem Trek Columbia Icefield

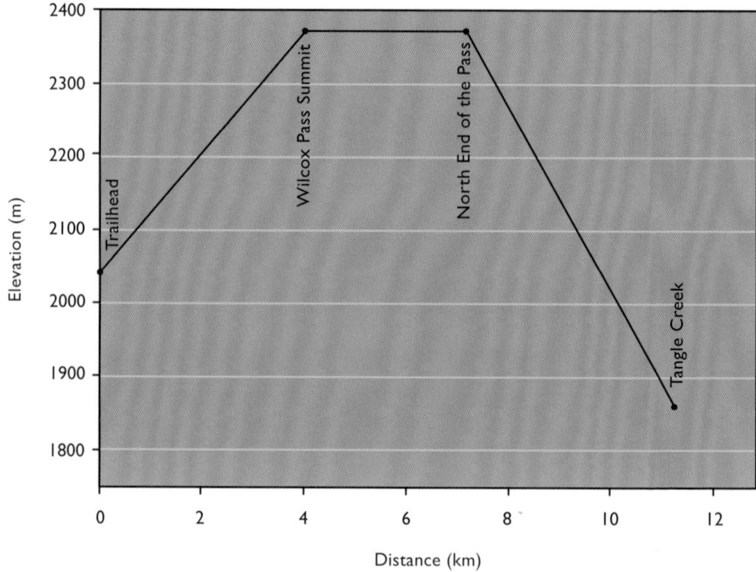

Trailhead

The south trailhead parking lot is on the north side of the Wilcox Creek Campground access road, approximately 50 m from the Icefields Parkway. The campground is 3 km south of the Icefields Centre or 2 km north of Sunwapta Pass at the Banff–Jasper Park boundary. The north trailhead is approximately 10 km along the parkway at Tangle Falls.

0.0 Trail climbs steadily through the forest.

0.6 First viewpoint looking out over the highway.

1.6 Out of the trees. The trail climbs along a ridge high above the highway. The terrain remains very open; watch for a flock of bighorn sheep in this area.

3.9 Top of the pass. The area is flat, open and very rocky with great views. A few cairns mark the route.

6.3 Cross a rock pile marked with cairns. The easy-to-follow trail continues along the left side of the valley, often marked with cairns.

7.2 North end of the pass. The trail starts to drop sharply.

8.0 Steep descent into the forest.

8.5 Trail is a well-beaten path following a small creek.

8.8 Cross the stream on a bridge. The trail climbs to the left side of the valley then drops again.

10.2 Remnants of an old log cabin. The trail soon drops very steeply into the Sunwapta valley, goes south and then turns north, probably on the old highway.

11.2 Tangle Creek trailhead and Tangle Falls.

Notes

Introduction

1 Qtd. in E.J. Hart, *Jimmy Simpson: Legend of the Rockies* (Canmore: Altitude, 1993), 168.

2 Ibid.

Route I

1 Jon Whyte, *Indians in the Rockies* (Canmore: Altitude, 1985), 24.

2 Barbara Huck and Doug Whiteway, *In Search of Ancient Alberta* (Winnipeg: Heartland Publications, 1988), 94. For a discussion of early occupation of the Bow Valley around present-day Banff townsite, see E.J. Hart, *The Place of Bows: Exploring the Heritage of the Banff-Bow Valley, Part 1 to 1930* (Banff: EJH Literary Enterprises Ltd., 1999), Chapter 1.

3 J.N. Wallace, "Early Explorations along the Bow and Saskatchewan Rivers," *Alberta Historical Review* 9:2 (1961), 12.

4 Gillean Daffern, *Canmore and Kananaskis: Short Walks for Inquiring Minds* (Calgary: Rocky Mountain Books, 1994), 67.

5 Wallace, 12. Wallace appears to have confused the yew, first described by David Douglas, with the well-known Douglas fir, named after David Douglas. In the book *Native Trees of Canada*, published by the Canada Department of Forestry in 1917 (page 2) the authors state that "the wood [of the Western yew] … is unexcelled for uses where resilience is important, such as for bows and canoe paddles."

6 Ernie Lakusta, *Canmore and Kananaskis History Explorer* (Canmore: Altitude, 2002), 20.

7 Eleanor G. Luxton, *Banff, Canada's First National Park: A History and a Memory of Rocky Mountains Park* (Banff: Summerthought, 1975), 27.

8 The first white men to enter the Rocky Mountains south of the Peace River were David Thompson and his party in the fall of 1800. For more details, see *Life of the Trail 1* (Calgary: Rocky Mountain Books, 2008), 22–29.

9 Lakusta, 9.

10 Joyce and Peter McCart, *On the Road with David Thompson* (Calgary: Fifth House, 2000), 31–40.

11 J.E.A. Macleod, "Peigan Post and the Blackfoot Trade," *Canadian Historical Review* 24 (1943): 273–79.

12 Ibid, 278.

13 J.N. Wallace, July 9, 1923, letter to J.E.A. Macleod, J.N. Wallace manuscript collection, Bruce Peel Special Collections Library, University of Alberta.

14 J.E.A. Macleod, "Old Bow Fort," *The Canadian Historical Review* 12 (1931), 411.

15 Ibid, 407.

16 Qtd. in Ernie Lakusta, *Banff and Lake Louise History Explorer* (Canmore: Altitude, 2004), 50–51.

17 J.H. Warre, *Overland to Oregon in 1845* (Ottawa: Public Archives of Canada, Information Canada, 1976), 34.

18 Qtd. in E.J. Hart, *The Place of Bows: Exploring the Heritage of the Banff–Bow Valley, Part 1 to 1930* (Banff: EJH Literary Enterprises, 1999), 48.

19 Luxton, 34.

20 For a brief biography of James Hector, see *Life of the Trail 1* (Calgary: Rocky Mountain Books, 2008), 74–76.

21 Bruce Haig, *Following Historic Trails: James Hector, Explorer* (Calgary: Detselig Enterprises, 1983), 8.

22 Qtd. in Edna (Hill) Appleby, *Canmore: The Story of an Era* (Canmore: Edna Appleby, 1975), 9.

23 Ibid.

24 Irene M. Spry, *The Palliser Expedition: The Dramatic Story of Western Canadian Exploration, 1857-1860*, 2nd edition (Saskatoon: Fifth House, 1995), 148.

25 Irene Spry, ed., *The Papers of the Palliser Expedition, 1857–1860* (Toronto: The Chamberlain Society, 1968), 295.

26 Hart, 1999, 46.

27 Spry, 1968, 295.

28 Richard Thomas Wright, *Overlanders: 1858 Gold* (Saskatoon: Western Producer Prairie Books, 1985), 110–111.

29 For a description of this trip see *Life of the Trail 1*, 72–73.

30 James Carnegie, Earl of Southesk, *Saskatchewan and the Rocky Mountains* (Rutland, VT: Charles E. Tuttle, 1969), 245.

31 J.N. Wallace, *Southesk's Journey through the West in 1859*, J.N. Wallace manuscript collection, Bruce Peel Special Collections Library, University of Alberta.

32 Wright, 136–39.

33 Beryl Hallworth and Monica Jackson, *Pioneer Naturalists of the Rocky Mountains and the Selkirks* (Calgary: Calgary Field Naturalists Society, 1985), 2.

34 For a brief biographical sketch of Tom Wilson, see *Life of the Trail 2* (Calgary: Rocky Mountain Books, 2008), 42–44.

35 Jon Whyte and Carol Harmon, *Lake Louise: A Diamond in the Wilderness* (Banff: Altitude, 1982), 9.

36 Rob Alexander and Dene Cooper, *Exshaw: Heart of the Valley* (Exshaw: Exshaw Historical Society, 2005), 79.

37 "Sir Sandford Fleming," *Canadian Alpine Journal* 1:1 (1907), 23.

38 Ibid.

39 Appleby, 26.

40 Alexander and Cooper, 79.

41 William Vaux, Notes from CPR trip 1894, June 28 to August 4, Vaux fonds, M107, Whyte Museum of the Canadian Rockies, file P16.

42 Ibid.

43 For a brief biography of Coleman, see *Life of the Trail 4: Historic Hikes in Eastern Jasper National Park* (Calgary: Rocky Mountain Books, 2009), 66–68.

44 Luxton, 53.

45 Ibid.

46 *Ralph Connor Memorial United Church, 1891–1892* (Canmore: Ralph Connor Memorial United Church Historical Committee, 1982).

47 For a brief biography of William Twin, see *Life of the Trail 1, 132–33.*

48 Parks Canada fonds, Whyte Museum of the Canadian Rockies, M317/4.

49 Bill Waiser, *Park Prisoners: The Untold Story of Canada's National Parks, 1915–1946* (Calgary: Fifth House, 1995), 12–45.

50 For a brief biography of Walcott, see *Life of the Trail 2*, 120–22.

51 Ellis L. Yochelson, *Smithsonian Institution Secretary: Charles Doolittle Walcott* (Kent, Ohio: Kent State University Press, 2000), 406.

52 Cliff Kopas, *Packhorses to the Pacific: A Wilderness Honeymoon* (Victoria: Touchwood Editions, 2004), 167.

53 Ibid, vii.

54 Ibid, 32.

55 Ibid.

56 Ibid.

Route II

1 E.J. Hart, *Jimmy Simpson: Legend of the Rockies* (Canmore: Altitude, 1993), 25.

2 Ibid, 26.

3 For a history of Howse Pass, see *Life of the Trail 2* (Calgary: Rocky Mountain Books, 2008), 23–61.

4 For more information on this trip, see *Life of the Trail 2*, 24–32.

5 This trip was erroneously recorded in a 1958 article as the first trip from Laggan to the North Saskatchewan River.

6 Laggan was the main starting point for trips north between 1885 and 1930, with the exception of the few that began from Field along the Amiskwi Pass trail (see *Life of the Trail 2*, 45–50).

7 E.J. Hart, *Diamond Hitch: The Early Outfitters and Guides of Banff and Jasper* (Banff: Summerthought, 1979), 10.

8 Philip S. Abbott, "The First Ascent of Mount Hector, Canadian Rockies," *Appalachia* 8:1 (1896), 2.

9 Ibid, 3.

10 Ibid, 3.

11 Ibid, 7.

12 Ibid.

13 Walter Wilcox, *Camping in the Canadian Rockies* (New York: G.P. Putnam and Sons, 1896), 186.

14 Ibid.

15 Ralph Edwards, *The Trail to the Charmed Land* (Victoria: Herbert R. Larsen, 1950), 86.

16 Ibid, 86–87.

17 Wilcox, 206.

18 For a description of the Sawback Range, see *Life of the Trail 1* (Calgary: Rocky Mountain Books, 2008), 129–40.

19 Wilcox, 186.

20 W.C. Taylor, *The Snows of Yesteryear: J. Norman Collie, Mountaineer* (Toronto: Holt, Rinehart and Winston of Canada, 1973), 93.

21 H.E.M. Stutfield and J. Norman Collie, *Climbs and Exploration in the Canadian Rockies* (Calgary: Aquila Books, 1998), 26.

22 Ibid, 27.

23 Ibid, 39.

24 Ibid, 40–41

25 Ibid, 41–42.

26 See *Life of the Trail 2*, 27–50.

27 Stanley Washburn, *Trails, Trappers and Tenderfeet in the New Empire Western Canada* (London: A. Melrose, 1912), 14.

28 Ibid.

29 For a description of the trip to Emerald Lake, see *Life of the Trail 2*, 96.

30 See *Life of the Trail 2*, 52.

31 For descriptions of Howse Pass and Glacier Lake, see *Life of the Trail 2*, 52.

32 Hart, 1993, 24–26.

33 Washburn, 59.

34 Ibid, 66.

35 Ibid, 59.

36 Ibid, 99.

37 For details of the trip up the Alexandra River, see *Life of the Trail 2*, 153–54.

38 James Outram, *In the Heart of the Canadian Rockies* (New York: Macmillan, 1905), 271–307.

39 Stutfield and Collie, 234–35.

40 Ibid, 246–47.

41 For a brief biography of Bridgland, see *Life of the Trail 1*, 48.

42 Esther Fraser, *Wheeler* (Banff: Summerthought, 1978), 57.

43 Hart, 1993, 37.

44 R.M. Patterson, *The Buffalo Head* (Victoria: Horsdal & Schubart, 1994), 173.

45 For a brief biography of Parker see *Life of the Trail 2*, 111–12.

46 Fraser, 115.

47 E.J. Hart, *Diamond Hitch: The Early Outfitters and Guides of Banff and Jasper* (Banff: Summerthought, 1979), 102.

48 For a recent biography of Mary Schäffer see Janice Sanford Beck, *No Ordinary Woman: The Story of Mary Schäffer Warren* (Calgary: Rocky Mountain Books, 2001).

49 Mary T.S. Schäffer, "Old Indian Trails: Expedition of 1907," *A Hunter of Peace*, ed. E.J. Hart (Banff: The Whyte Foundation, 1980), 49.

50 See *Life of the Trail 1*, 104.

51 See *Life of the Trail 1*, 104–05.

52 Schäffer, "Old Indian Trails: Expedition of 1907," 23.

53 Ibid, 50.

54 Mary T.S. Schäffer, "Old Indian Trails: Expedition of 1908," *A Hunter of Peace*, ed. E.J. Hart (Banff: The Whyte Foundation, 1980), 82.

55 Ibid, 86.

56 Hart, 1993, 66–67.

57 For more details of this camp, see *Life of the Trail 2*, 116.

58 For a brief biography of Hickson, see *Life of the Trail 1*, 37–39.

59 J.W.A. Hickson, "Notes of a Trip to the Saskatchewan River and Freshfield Glacier (1913)" *Canadian Alpine Journal* VI (1914), 93.

60 Ibid, 95–96.

61 See *Life of the Trail 2*, 28.

62 See *Life of the Trail 2*, 45–50.

63 See *Life of the Trail 2*, 166.

64 For details of this trip see *Life of the Trail 1*, 91–92.

65 Wilson fonds, Whyte Museum of the Canadian Rockies, M10/1.

66 Ibid.

67 Ibid.

68 Robert Frothingham, "Big Horn on the Brazeau," *Field and Stream* 11 (March 1917), 385–87.

69 For a brief biography of Charles Walcott see *Life of the Trail 2*, 120–22.

70 For more information on the Off the Beaten Track Tours, see *Life of the Trail 1*, 54–56, and *Life of the Trail 2*, 58–60.

71 Joan Robson, *The Glacier Trail: Jasper to Lake Louise*, July 3 to 23, 1927, Robson family fonds, Jasper Yellowhead Museum and Archives, 993.37.5, 1–3.

72 Ibid, 4.

73 Ibid.

74 Ibid.

75 Hart, 1993, 128.

76 For further detail about these trips, see *Life of the Trail 2*, 56, 164–65.

77 J. Monroe Thorington, "A Mountaineering Journey through Jasper Park," *Canadian Alpine Journal* 16 (1928), 86–107.

78 Hart 1993, 144–45.

79 For details of this trip, see *Life of the Trail 2*, 171.

80 W.D. Rubinstein, "The Secret of Leopold Amery," *Historical Research* 73: 181 (June 2000), 175–196.

81 Cliff Kopas, *Packhorses to the Pacific: A Wilderness Honeymoon* (Victoria: TouchWood Editions, 2004), 40–41.

82 Ibid, 42.

83 For more details about the Castleguard Meadows trip, see *Life of the Trail 2*, 172.

84 Lorne and Kim Tetarenko, *Ken Jones: Mountain Man* (Calgary: Rocky Mountain Books, 1996), 74.

85 Stutfield and Collie, 241.

86 Ibid.

87 J. Monroe Thorington, *The Glittering Mountains of Canada* (Philadelphia: John W. Lea, 1925), 9.

Route III

1 A.P. Coleman, *The Canadian Rockies New & Old Trails* (Calgary: Aquila Books, 1999), 13–120.

2 Ibid, 170.

3 Ibid, 171.

4 Ibid, 189.

5 Ibid, 192.

6 Ibid.

7 Ibid.

8 Ibid, 193

9 Ibid.

10 Ibid, 196.

11 The Coleman party calculated that the height of Mount Brown was just over nine thousand feet, not the 16 to 17 thousand estimated by David Douglas.

12 H.E.M. Stutfield and J. Norman Collie, *Climbs and Exploration in the Canadian Rockies* (Calgary: Aquila Books, 1998), 71–72.

13 Ibid, 73.

14 For more information on the Pipestone Pass trip, see *Life of the Trail 1* (Calgary: Rocky Mountain Books, 2008), 85–89.

15 Stutfield and Collie, 93.

16 Ibid.

17 Ibid, 98.

18 Ibid.

19 For a brief biographical sketch of Jean Habel, see *Life of the Trail 2* (Calgary: Rocky Mountain Books, 2008), 88–90.

20 See *Life of the Trail 2*, 86–92.

21 Jean Habel, "The North Fork of the Wapta," *Appalachia* 8:4 (March 1898), 327–36.

22 E.J. Hart, *Diamond Hitch: The Early Outfitters and Guides of Banff and Jasper* (Banff: Summerthought, 1979), 62.

23 Ibid.

24 Ibid, 58.

25 Mary T.S. Schäffer, *Old Indian Trails of the Canadian Rockies* (Calgary: Rocky Mountain Books, 2007), 3.

26 Ibid, 15.

27 Ibid, 17.

28 Ibid, 18.

29 See *Life of the Trail 1*, 168–79.

30 See *Life of the Trail 1*, 72–112.

31 See *Life of the Trail 1*, 105–109, for details of the Laggan to Kootenay Plains portion of the trip.

32 Schäffer, 50.

33 Coleman, 251.

34 Ibid.

35 Stanley Washburn, *Trails, Trappers and Tenderfeet in the New Empire Western Canada* (London: A. Melrose, 1912), 125.

36 Ibid, 162.

37 Esther Fraser, *The Canadian Rockies: Early Travels and Explorations* (Edmonton: Hurtig, 1969), 225.

38 Whyte Foundation, *Great Days in the Rockies: The Photographs of Byron Harmon, 1906–1934* (Banff: Altitude, 1984), 13.

39 Esther Fraser, *Wheeler* (Banff: Summerthought, 1978), 115.

40 E.J. Hart, *Jimmy Simpson: Legend of the Rockies* (Canmore: Altitude, 1993), 141.

41 See *Life of the Trail 1*, 54–56, and *Life of the Trail 2*, 58–60, for more information on Hinman's tours.

42 Allen Carpe, "The Clemenceau Group," *Canadian Alpine Journal* 13 (1923), 79–92.

43 F.N. Waterman, "From Field to Mount Robson–Summer 1923," *Canadian Alpine Journal* 14 (1924),

113–22. See *Life of the Trail 2*, 57 and 165, for more details of this trip.

44 Lewis R. Freeman, *On the Roof of the Rockies: The Great Columbia Icefield of the Canadian Rockies* (Toronto: McClelland and Stewart, 1925), 17.

45 See *Life of the Trail 2*, 169, for details of this portion of the trip.

46 Zac Robinson, "The Golden Years of Mountaineering in Canada," *Culturing Wilderness in Jasper National Park*, ed. I.S. MacLaren (Edmonton: University of Alberta Press, 2007), 274–79.

47 A.J. Ostheimer, *Every Other Day: The Journals of the Remarkable Rocky Mountain Climbs and Explorations of A.J. Ostheimer*, ed. R.W. Sandford and Jon Whelan (Canmore: Alpine Club of Canada, 2002), 13.

48 For a brief biography of Mona Harragin, see *Life of the Trail 4: Historic Hikes in Eastern Jasper National Park* (Calgary: Rocky Mountain Books, 2009), 115–17.

49 Cliff Kopas, *Packhorses to the Pacific: A Wilderness Honeymoon* (Victoria: TouchWood Editions, 2004), 55–66.

50 Ibid, 174.

51 See *Life of the Trail 2*, 164–65.

Image Credits

Page 20 Peigan Post was built on the Bow River in 1832. This is an artist's conception of what the fort would have looked like. The fort was abandoned in 1834 and subsequently burned. The remains of Peigan Post became known as Old Bow Fort. (Courtesy Buffalo Nations Luxton Museum, Banff)

Page 28 David Thompson, geographer, surveyor and map maker, took celestial observations wherever he went. He later used the data collected to draw remarkably accurate maps of the Northwest. (Sketch by C.W. Jefferys, taken from C.W. Jefferys, *The Picture Gallery of Canadian History, Volume II* [The Ryerson Press, Toronto: 1945], 146)

Page 30 This sketch of Old Bow Fort indicates the locations of the 11 chimneys that were visible to historian J.N. Wallace in 1924. (J.N. Wallace, 1924, University of Alberta)

Page 35 Sir George Simpson, governor of the Hudson's Bay Company between 1826 and 1860, was one of the first non-Natives to enter the mountains through Devil's Gap. He was the first to comment on the four lakes that followed the gap: the three Ghost Lakes and Lake Minnewanka. (Library and Archives Canada, C-044702)

Page 35 Red River Métis James Sinclair led a party of settlers from the Winnipeg area to Oregon's Pacific Coast. (Royal British Columbia Museum and BC Archives, A-01741)

Page 38 Jesuit missionary Father Pierre Jean de Smet entered the Bow Valley through White Man Gap after having crossed White Man Pass. He travelled very little in the Bow Valley. (Glenbow Museum and Archives, NA-1391-1)

Page 40 Reverend Robert Rundle, who briefly entered the mountains along the Bow in 1844 and 1847, had the mountain between Canmore and Banff named in his honour, although he did not climb it. (Glenbow Museum and Archives, NA-642-1)

Page 44 Peter Erasmus, son of a Danish man and an Ojibwa mixed-blood woman, was a man of many talents who became a legend within his own lifetime. (Glenbow Museum and Archives, NA-319-1)

Page 44 Palliser Expedition botanist Eugene Bourgeau travelled along the Bow River with the Hector party only as far as Lac des Arcs, where he collected a large number of alpine specimens. (Saskatchewan Archives Board, R-A 4982)

Page 49 James Carnegie, Earl of Southesk, travelled through the mountains for pleasure and the pursuit of large game. He and Hector's party nearly crossed paths in the Bow Valley. (Glenbow Museum and Archives, NA-1355-2)

Page 55 Professor John Macoun was a botanist, explorer and naturalist who travelled widely in Western Canada, collecting specimens for the Geological Survey of Canada. (Glenbow Museum and Archives, NA-3840-5)

Page 58 Best known for his toughness and unparalleled proficiency with foul language, Rogers is honoured today for his discovery of the pass that bears his name. (Glenbow Museum and Archives, NA-1949-1)

Page 60 Coal was discovered in Canmore (Siding 27) in 1884. The town grew up on both sides of the river: "townside" and "mineside." This 1907 image shows the "mineside" area, south of the river. (Whyte Museum of the Canadian Rockies, NA-66-2443)

Page 60 The coal-mining town of Anthracite (Siding 28) grew up at the junction of the Cascade and Bow rivers, near the base of Cascade Mountain, in 1887. Ten years later, the mine (located in a ravine captured on the right side of this photo) closed and Anthracite became a ghost town. Today the area is overgrown, and the course of the river altered. The town site's former location is marked by the Cascade Power Plant and surge tower. (Glenbow Museum and Archives, NA-573-9)

Page 62 Sir Sandford Fleming was an extremely gifted man who served as engineer-in-chief for the construction of the CPR. He is perhaps best known today as the person who invented international standard time. (Library and Archives Canada, CIN 3962)

Page 64 Siding 29, the original site of the Town of Banff, grew up near the base of Cascade Mountain, close to where the airstrip is today. (Whyte Museum of the Canadian Rockies, V527/PS-229)

Page 64 Joe Smith, the bachelor hermit of Silver City, settled before the boom and stayed on another 52 years after the town disappeared. As Smith got on in years, residents of Banff and Lake Louise who passed by would make sure smoke was rising from his chimney – a sign that all was well. (Glenbow Museum and Archives, NA-163-1)

Page 64 In 1884 the boom town of Silver City grew almost overnight at the base of Castle Mountain. It died almost as quickly the following year. (Glenbow Museum and Archives, NA-3188-12)

Page 65 Unlike other towns along the railway, Exshaw (shown here in 1908) was neither a railroad town nor a mining town. Its economic base is cement manufacture, and the town continues to thrive. (Whyte Museum of the Canadian Rockies, NA-66-2450)

Page 68 The Twin brothers, William and Joshua, were Stoneys who cleared trails and carried out other tasks in the early days of settlement in the mountains. Much of their work was for the CPR, but in this case they were working for outfitter Tom Wilson. They had strong ties with the Brewster family of Banff. (Glenbow Museum and Archives, NA-7-175)

Page 69 Internees from the Castle Mountain internment camp helped build the motor road from Banff to Lake Louise during World War I. Workers shown here are using hand tools only. (Glenbow Museum and Archives, Millican Collection, NA-1870-77)

Page 70 Annie Staple, the first gatekeeper for Rocky Mountains Park, continued to work at the park entrance through its three relocations over the course of her lengthy career. (Whyte Museum of the Canadian Rockies, NA-66-2472)

Page 72 Reverend Charles Gordon, known widely as Ralph Connor, the author of romantic accounts of life in the North-West, was an accomplished musician and dedicated Christian minister. (Photographed by Arnold Climo, St. John, NB; courtesy Mary Smith)

Page 74 A 1921 view of the eastern entrance to Rocky Mountains Park, near Exshaw, where Annie Staple, a widowed warden's wife, acted as 24-hour gatekeeper. The G and R on the sides of the gate stand for "George Rex," King George V. (Whyte Museum of the Canadian Rockies, V263/NA-71-3436)

Page 90 James Hector of the Palliser Expedition was the first non-Aboriginal man to cross from the Bow River drainage to that of the North Saskatchewan. All of the expedition's explorations north of the Bow were done by Hector and his party. The unfortunate kick Hector received from his horse, which led to the naming of the Kicking Horse River, did not slow him down. (Glenbow Museum and Archives, NA-659-62)

Page 92 Later in his career, Tom Wilson established a trading post on the Kootenay Plains. He is shown here in front of the cabin where he lived alone for several winters. (Whyte Museum of the Canadian Rockies, V701/LC-36)

Page 94 Appalachian Mountain Club member Philip Abbot, recognized as one of the foremost mountaineers in the United States at that time, was the first person to die in a climbing accident in the Canadian Rockies. His ill-fated ascent of Mount Lefroy took place in August 1896. (Whyte Museum of the Canadian Rockies, NA-66-1981)

Page 95 Walter Wilcox was one of the first non-Aboriginal people to explore the route north from Laggan to Bow Summit and Sunwapta Pass and the Athabasca drainage. The route he followed around the Athabasca glacier bears his name. Wilcox spent many summers in the Canadian Rockies, exploring as far south as the Mount Assiniboine area. He is shown here with (l–r) Stoney John Hunter and outfitter Tom Wilson. (Whyte Museum of the Canadian Rockies, NA-66-1981)

Page 97 The Fay party at Laggan in 1897. (l–r) Charles S. Thompson, Charles E. Fay, unknown, Harold B. Dixon (seated), unknown, unknown, J. Norman Collie (with pipe), Hershel C. Parker and Peter Sarbach. The unidentified men include A. Michael and C.L. Noyes. (Whyte Museum of the Canadian Rockies, V653/NG-4-278)

Page 99 (l–r) Peter Sarbach, George Baker and J. Norman Collie relaxing in Banff before beginning their 1897 trip. (Whyte Museum of the Canadian Rockies, V701/LC-90)

Page 107 Alpine surveying involved a great deal of mountaineering, and surveyors were actively involved in founding the Alpine Club of Canada. Some of the founding group, shown here: (l–r, back row) unknown; Jack Otto, outfitter; A.O. Wheeler, surveyor, president; Tom Wilson, outfitter; S.H. Mitchell; R. Campbell, outfitter. (l–r, front row) Dan Campbell, outfitter; M.P. Bridgland, surveyor and chief mountaineer; unknown; Reverend J.C. Herdman; A.P. Coleman, explorer and mountaineer, vice-president. (Whyte Museum of the Canadian Rockies, V701/LC-32)

Page 110 Surveyor, mountaineer and author Arthur Wheeler is best known as the co-founder of the Alpine Club of Canada. This famous stance is known as the "he who must be obeyed" pose. (Whyte Museum of the Canadian Rockies, M-517-72)

Page 111 Outfitters in the early days were men of many talents. In this photograph, Jimmy Simpson is catching butterflies for renowned collector Mary de la Beach-Nichol. (Whyte Museum of the Canadian Rockies, NA-66-468)

Page 113 Mary Schäffer and guide Billy Warren (shown here), together with Mollie Adams and packer Sid Unwin, travelled widely in the Rocky Mountains in the first decade of the twentieth century. Schäffer and Warren later married. (Whyte Museum of the Canadian Rockies, V439/PS-6)

Page 115 Wildlife artist Carl Rungius first came to the Canadian Rockies at the invitation of outfitter Jimmy Simpson and ended up residing in Banff for part of each year thereafter. (Glenbow Museum and Archives, NA-3466-58)

Page 119 Jimmy Simpson came to Canada at age 19 and established himself as a guide, outfitter, hunter, builder and lover of the arts. (Glenbow Museum and Archives, NA-3466-20, ca. 1910)

Page 121 Canadian J.W.A. Hickson was a prolific mountaineer who claimed more than 30 first ascents during his career. (Whyte Museum of the Canadian Rockies, V14/ACOOP/86)

Page 123 John Wilson (l) stands with his father, Tom Wilson, in front of one of Wilson's winter cabins on the Kootenay Plains. (Glenbow Museum and Archives, NA-1263-2)

Page 123 (l–r) Bess Wilson, Jen (who later married John Wilson), and Dora Wilson in Banff in 1916. They accompanied John Wilson to the Kootenay Plains to see the old ranch where their father used to live during the winter. (Whyte Museum of the Canadian Rockies, V701/LC-155)

Page 125 Mary Vaux Walcott spent nearly every summer from 1894 to 1940 in the Canadian Rockies. Although her early life was burdened with looking after her father, she later spent her summers travelling with her husband, Dr. Charles Walcott, painting and photographing wildflowers. (Glenbow Museum and Archives, NA-529-5)

Page 125 Caroline Hinman made a career of escorting teenaged girls on outfitted trips through the Canadian Rockies. Jim Boyce was her preferred guide, and Hinman went to great lengths to see that his hired men were kept away from her young charges. (Whyte Museum of the Canadian Rockies, V282/PD10 p 47)

Page 127 Jasper outfitter Jack Brewster started his Glacier Tours from Jasper to Lake Louise in 1923 but was hard hit by the Depression in 1929. (Jasper–Yellowhead Museum and Archives, PA-34-17)

Page 128 J. Monroe Thorington (r) with climbing guide Conrad Kain on top of Trapper Peak in 1933. (Whyte Museum of the Canadian Rockies, NA-66-1778)

Page 130 World traveller Leopold Amery (r) managed to climb the mountain that was named in his honour. He is shown here on the summit with Swiss guide Edward Feuz Jr. (Whyte Museum of the Canadian Rockies, NA-66-2117)

Page 133 Ken Jones (l) with Elizabeth Rummel, heading for Skoki Lodge in 1945. Jones was the first licensed Canadian mountain guide, and in his spare time, he helped his friends run backcountry lodges. Skoki Lodge was built in the early 1930s as a ski lodge. (Whyte Museum of the Canadian Rockies, NA-66-1108)

Page 146 This pencil drawing of botanist David Douglas was executed by his niece, Miss Atkinson. Douglas crossed Athabasca Pass in 1827 and started a controversy that took mountaineers 66 years to solve. (Whyte Museum of the Canadian Rockies, M-106-7)

Page 148 Professor, geologist, explorer and mountaineer A.P. Coleman set out to locate and climb Mount Brown, thus resolving the "David Douglas controversy." (Whyte Museum of the Canadian Rockies, detail from V14/AC33 P/3)

Page 151 The old fur trading post of Jasper House, located along the Athabasca River east of the town of Jasper. This is how it appeared to Charles Horetzky, a member of Sandford Fleming's survey team, on January 15, 1872. (Glenbow Museum and Archives, NA-382-5)

Page 157 Professor Jean Habel explored extensively in the areas around Yoho Valley and Fortress Lake during his two summers in the Rockies. (Whyte Museum of the Canadian Rockies, V14/AC-175 P-1)

Page 158 Members of the first party to travel the entire distance from Banff to Jasper are (l–r standing): Bob Logan, Sid Collins, Phil Moore, George Harrison and Jim Brewster; and (l–r seated) Fred Tabuteau and Halsey Williams. (Whyte Museum of the Canadian Rockies, NA-66-50)

Page 159 Mary Schäffer and Mollie Adams, the first non-Aboriginal women to venture far into the wilds of the Rocky Mountains, were not averse to bringing along some small comforts from civilization. They are shown here pumping up air mattresses. (Whyte Museum of the Canadian Rockies, V527/NA-102)

Page 163 (l–r) Reverend George Kinney and Lucius Coleman on the main glacier, Mount Robson. Lucius Coleman travelled with his brother, A.P. Coleman, on most of his trips in the Rocky Mountains; his Morley ranch supplied the majority of the outfit. (Whyte Museum of the Canadian Rockies, 02.6 C67, p 335)

Page 166 Mary Schäffer's second trip in search of *Chaba Imne* (Maligne Lake) was aided by a map drawn from memory by Sampson Beaver, who had visited the lake as a boy. Even with the map, Schaffer's party had some difficulty locating the lake. (Whyte Museum of the Canadian Rockies, V 527/PS-53)

Page 169 Members of the 1911 ACC–Smithsonian expedition (l–r) James Shand-Harvey, Reverend George Kinney, Conrad Kain and Curly Phillips resting in camp before the latter three set out for Laggan. The remaining members of the party are (l–r) Charles Walcott Jr., Harry Blagden, Ned Hollister,

J.H. Riley and Arthur Wheeler. (Whyte Museum of the Canadian Rockies, v 263/NA-1148)

Page 172 Bryon Harmon was a renowned Banff photographer who set himself the task of photographing most of the major peaks in the Canadian Rockies. (Whyte Museum of the Canadian Rockies, NA-66-1949)

Page 176 When Lewis Freeman and Byron Harmon travelled from Lake Louise to Jasper in 1924, they brought carrier pigeons along for the ride. Though the pigeons belonged to Harmon, Freeman is shown here releasing one. (Whyte Museum of the Canadian Rockies, v263/NA-71 2278)

Page 178 The Japanese and Swiss alpinists who conquered Mount Alberta: (l–r) photographer Nagatane Okabe, geologist and geographer Masanobu Hatano, botanist and artist Yukio Mita, expedition doctor Tanezo Hayakawa, expedition secretary Seiichi Hashimoto, leader Yuko Maki, outfitter Fred Brewster, Jasper Park Lodge mountain guide Heinrich Fuhrer, Swiss amateur climber Jean Weber and Jasper Park Lodge mountain guide Hans Kohler. (Jasper–Yellowhead Museum and Archives, 17-3)

Page 180 Park Warden Charlie Matheson at his Brazeau Lake Warden Cabin in the 1920s. Matheson later married Mona Harragin, one of the first two licensed female guides in Canada's national parks. (Jasper–Yellowhead Museum and Archives, PA 54/13)

Page 181 Cliff and Ruth Kopas travelled overland from Calgary to Bella Coola on the Pacific Coast, hitting many of the scenic spots in the Rockies along the way. Cliff is seen here after arriving in Bella Coola, and Ruth is en route on Dream, a gentle pack horse that became an ideal

All other photographs: Emerson Sanford

Bibliography

Abbott, Philip S. "The First Ascent of Mount Hector, Canadian Rockies." *Appalachia* 8:1 (1896): 1–17.

Appleby, Edna (Hill). *Canmore: The Story of an Era.* Canmore: Edna Appleby, 1975.

Alexander, Rob and Dene Cooper. *Exshaw: Heart of the Valley.* Exshaw: Exshaw Historical Society, 2005.

Carpe, Allen. "The Clemenceau Group." *Canadian Alpine Journal* 13 (1923): 79–92.

Coleman, A.P. *The Canadian Rockies: New & Old Trails.* Calgary: Aquila Books, 1999.

Daffern, Gillean. *Canmore and Kananaskis: Short Walks for Inquiring Minds.* Calgary: Rocky Mountain Books, 1994.

Edwards, Ralph. *The Trail to the Charmed Land.* Victoria: Herbert R. Larsen, 1950.

Fairley, Bruce, ed. *The Canadian Mountaineering Anthology.* Edmonton: Lone Pine, 1994.

Fleming, Sir Sandford. "Memories of the Mountain." *Canadian Alpine Journal* 1:1 (1907): 9–34.

Fraser, Esther. *The Canadian Rockies: Early Travels and Explorations.* Edmonton: Hurtig, 1969.

Fraser, Esther. *Wheeler.* Banff: Summerthought, 1978.

Freeman, Lewis R. *On the Roof of the Rockies: The Great Columbia Icefield of the Canadian Rockies.* Toronto: McClelland and Stewart, 1925.

Frothingham, Robert. "Big Horn on the Brazeau." *Field and Stream* 11 (March 1917): 385–87.

Glenbow Museum. *Carl Rungius: Artist and Sportsman.* Toronto: Warwick, 2001.

Habel, Jean. "The North Fork of the Wapta." *Appalachia* 8:4 (March 1898): 327–36.

Haig, Bruce. *Following Historic Trails: James Hector, Explorer.* Calgary: Detselig Enterprises, 1983.

Hallworth, Beryl and Monica Jackson. *Pioneer Naturalists of the Rocky Mountains and the Selkirks.* Calgary: Calgary Field Naturalists Society, 1985.

Hart, E.J. *Diamond Hitch: The Early Outfitters and Guides of Banff and Jasper.* Banff: Summerthought, 1979.

Hart, E.J. *Jimmy Simpson: Legend of the Rockies.* Canmore: Altitude, 1993.

Hart, E.J. *The Place of Bows: Exploring the Heritage of the Banff-Bow Valley, Part I to 1930.* Banff: EJH Literary Enterprises, 1999.

Hickson, J.W.A. "Notes of a Trip to the Saskatchewan River and Freshfield Glacier (1913)." *Canadian Alpine Journal* VI (1914): 93–98.

Huck, Barbara and Doug Whiteway. *In Search of Ancient Alberta.* Winnipeg: Heartland, 1998.

J.N. Wallace manuscript collection. Bruce Peel Special Collections Library. University of Alberta. Edmonton, Alberta.

Kopas, Cliff. *Packhorses to the Pacific: A Wilderness Honeymoon.* Victoria: TouchWood Editions, 2004.

Lakusta, Ernie. *Banff and Lake Louise History Explorer.* Canmore: Altitude, 2004.

Lakusta, Ernie. *Canmore and Kananaskis History Explorer.* Canmore: Altitude, 2002.

Luxton, Eleanor G. *Banff, Canada's First National Park: A History and a Memory of Rocky Mountains Park.* Banff: Summerthought, 1975.

Macleod, J.E.A. "Old Bow Fort." *Canadian Historical Review* 12 (1931): 407–11.

Macleod, J.E.A. "Peigan Post and the Blackfoot Trade." *Canadian Historical Review* 24 (1943): 273–79.

McCart, Joyce and Peter. *On the Road with David Thompson.* Calgary: Fifth House, 2000.

Ostheimer, A.J. *Every Other Day: The Journals of the Remarkable Rocky Mountain Climbs and Explorations of A.J. Ostheimer.* Edited by R.W. Sandford and Jon Whelan. Canmore: Alpine Club of Canada, 2002.

Outram, James. *In the Heart of the Canadian Rockies.* New York: Macmillan, 1906.

Parks Canada fonds. Whyte Museum of the Canadian Rockies. Banff, Alberta. M317.

Patterson, R.M. *The Buffalo Head.* Victoria: Horsdal & Schubart, 1994.

Ralph Connor Memorial United Church, 1891–1892. Canmore: Ralph Connor Memorial United Church Historical Committee, 1982.

Robinson, Zac. "The Golden Years of Mountaineering in Canada." In *Culturing Wilderness in Jasper National Park.* Edited by I.S.

MacLaren. Edmonton: University of Alberta Press, 2007.

Robson, Joan. *The Glacier Trail: Jasper to Lake Louise, July 3 to 23, 1927*. Robson family fonds. Jasper Yellowhead Museum and Archives, 993.37.5.

Rubinstein, W.D. "The Secret of Leopold Amery." *Historical Research* 73: 181 (June 2000): 175–96.

Sanford Beck, Janice. *No Ordinary Woman: The Story of Mary Schäffer Warren*. Calgary: Rocky Mountain Books, 2001.

Schäffer, Mary T.S. "Old Indian Trails: Expedition of 1907." In *A Hunter of Peace: Mary T.S. Schäffer's Old Indian Trails of the Canadian Rockies*. Edited and annotated by E.J. Hart. Banff: The Whyte Foundation, 1980.

Schäffer, Mary T.S. "Old Indian Trails: Expedition of 1908." In *A Hunter of Peace: Mary T. S. Schäffer's Old Indian Trails of the Canadian Rockies*. Edited and annotated by E.J. Hart. Banff: The Whyte Foundation, 1980.

Schäffer, Mary T.S. *Old Indian Trails of the Canadian Rockies*. Calgary: Rocky Mountain Books, 2007.

Schaldach, William J. *Carl Rungius: Big Game Hunter*. Vermont: The Countryman Press, 1945.

Southesk, James Carnegie, Earl of. *Saskatchewan and the Rocky Mountains*. Rutland, VT: Charles E. Tuttle Co., 1969.

Spry, Irene M. *The Palliser Expedition: The Dramatic Story of Western Canadian Exploration, 1857-1860*, 2nd edition. Saskatoon: Fifth House, 1995.

Spry, Irene, ed. *The Papers of the Palliser Expedition, 1857–1860*. Toronto: The Champlain Society, 1968.

Stutfield, H.E.M. and J. Norman Collie. *Climbs and Exploration in the Canadian Rockies*. Calgary: Aquila Books, 1998.

Taylor, W.C. *The Snows of Yesteryear: J. Norman Collie, Mountaineer*. Toronto: Holt, Rinehart and Winston of Canada, 1973.

Tetarenko, Lorne and Kim. *Ken Jones: Mountain Man*. Calgary: Rocky Mountain Books, 1996.

Thorington, J. Monroe. "A Mountaineering Journey through Jasper Park." *Canadian Alpine Journal* 16 (1928): 86–107.

Vaux family fonds. Whyte Museum of the Canadian Rockies. Banff, Alberta. M107. P16.

Waiser, Bill. *Park Prisoners: The Untold Story of Canada's National Parks, 1915–1946*. Calgary: Fifth House, 1995.

Wallace, J.N. "Early Explorations along the Bow and Saskatchewan Rivers." *Alberta Historical Review* 9:2 (1961): 12–21.

Warre, H.J. *Overland to Oregon in 1845*. Ottawa: Public Archives of Canada, Information Canada, 1976.

Washburn, Stanley. *Trails, Trappers and Tenderfeet in the New Empire Western Canada*. London: A. Melrose, 1912.

Waterman, F.N. "From Field to Mount Robson–Summer 1923." *Canadian Alpine Journal* 14 (1924): 113–22.

Whyte Foundation. *Great Days in the Rockies: The Photographs of Byron Harmon, 1906–1934*. Banff: Altitude, 1984.

Whyte, Jon. *Indians in the Rockies*. Canmore: Altitude, 1985.

Whyte, Jon and Carol Harmon. *Lake Louise: A Diamond in the Wilderness*. Banff: Altitude, 1982.

Wilcox, Walter. *Camping in the Canadian Rockies*. New York: G.P. Putnam and Sons, 1896.

Wilson fonds. Whyte Museum of the Canadian Rockies. Banff, Alberta. M10/1.

Wilson, Thomas E. *Trailblazer of the Canadian Rockies*. Calgary: Glenbow-Alberta Institute, 1972.

Wright, Richard Thomas. *Overlanders: 1858 Gold*. Saskatoon: Western Producer Prairie Books, 1985.

Yochelson, Ellis L. *Smithsonian Institution Secretary: Charles Doolittle Walcott*. Ohio: Kent State University Press, 2000.

Index

About the Authors

Emerson Sanford, originally from Nova Scotia, first visited the mountains of western Canada in the summer of 1961. Eleven years later, he moved to Alberta and has been hiking ever since. After beginning to backpack seriously with his teenaged daughters in 1990, he began to wonder who cut the trails and how their routing had been determined. Since then, not only has he delved through printed material about the trails, he has also solo hiked every historic route and most long trails between Mount Robson and the Kananaskis Lakes – over 3000 kilometres over five years! Emerson now lives in Canmore with his wife, Cheryl.

Janice Sanford Beck is the author of the best-selling *No Ordinary Woman: the Story of Mary Schäffer Warren* (Rocky Mountain Books, 2001). She has also written the introduction to the latest edition of Mary T.S. Schäffer's *Old Indian Trails of the Canadian Rockies* (Rocky Mountain Books, 2007) and, with Cheryl Sanford, researched the Mary Schäffer Warren portion of the Glenbow Museum's new permanent exhibit, *Mavericks*. Janice is presently masquerading as a flatlander, making her home in Saskatoon with her partner, Shawn, and their three children.

Further Reading …

Life of the Trail 1

Historic Hikes in Eastern Banff National Park

Emerson Sanford & Janice Sanford Beck

Life of the Trail 1: Historic Hikes in Eastern Banff National Park follows the trails of David Thompson, Walter Wilcox, the Palliser Expedition, James Carnegie Earl of Southesk, Bill Peyto and A.P. Coleman. Along the way, the reader will journey from the Kootenay Plains to Lake Minnewanka, discovering the stories behind routes through the mountain towns of Banff and Lake Louise and along the Red Deer, Ptarmigan and Skoki valleys.

ISBN 978-1-894765-99-2

Colour and Black & White Photos, Maps

$26.95, Softcover

Life of the Trail 2

Historic Hikes in Northern Yoho National Park

Emerson Sanford & Janice Sanford Beck

Life of the Trail 2: Historic Hikes in Northern Yoho National Park follows the trails of fur traders La Gasse and Le Blanc, the Palliser Expedition, Tom Wilson, J.J. McArthur, Professor Jean Habel, Walter Wilcox, C.S. Thompson, David Thompson, Jimmy Simpson and Jack Brewster. Along the way, the reader will journey past pristine lakes and glaciers that have become legendary throughout the world, discovering the stories behind routes through the mountain towns of Lake Louise and Field; over Howse, Amiskwi, Bow and Burgess passes; and along Yoho, Emerald and Castleguard rivers.

ISBN 978-1-897522-00-4

Colour and Black & White Photos, Maps

$26.95, Softcover

LIFE OF THE TRAIL 4

Historic Hikes in Eastern Jasper National Park

Emerson Sanford & Janice Sanford Beck

Life of the Trail 4: Historic Hikes in Eastern Jasper National Park includes trails throughout the Jasper area, as well as routes in the White Goat Wilderness and part of the Bighorn Wildland, outside the national park. The main routes are fur-trade routes: Duncan McGillivray's route along the Brazeau river and Poboktan Creek, Jacques Cardinal's route from Jasper to the North Saskatchewan River along the South Boundary Trail and over Job Pass, and Old Klyne's Trail over Maligne and Cataract passes and along the Cline River to the Kootenay Plains. The fourth is a 20th century route, the Skyline Trail.

ISBN 978-1-897522-42-2
Colour and Black & White Photos, Maps
$26.95, Softcover

The Canadian Rockies: New and Old Trails

Mountain Classics Collection 1

A.P. Coleman
Foreword by Chic Scott

First published in 1911, this book gives modern-day readers a glimpse of the early days of mountaineering in the Canadian West. It paints a sympathetic picture of the rugged men and women who opened the region and of the hardships they endured.

ISBN 978-1-897522-50-9
Black & White Photos
$19.95, Softcover

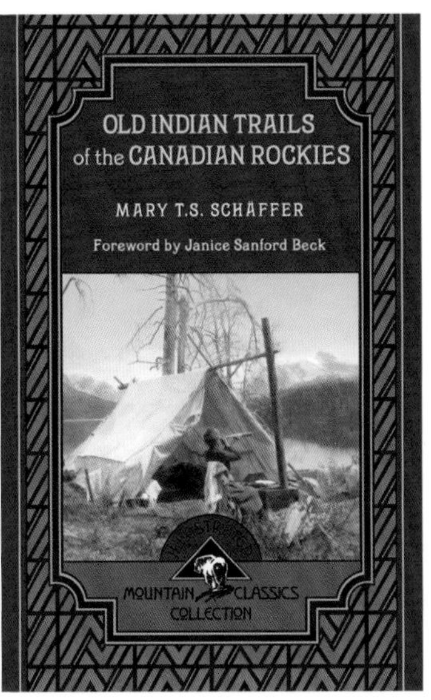

Old Indian Trails of the Canadian Rockies

Mountain Classics Collection 2

Mary T.S. Schäffer
Foreword by Janice Sanford Beck

Mary T.S. Schäffer was an avid explorer and one of the first non-Native women to venture into the heart of the Canadian Rocky Mountains, where few women – or men – had gone before. First published in 1911, *Old Indian Trails of the Canadian Rockies* is Schäffer's story of her adventures in the traditionally male-dominated world of climbing and exploration.

ISBN 978-1-897522-49-3
Black & White Photos
$19.95 Softcover

In the Heart of the Canadian Rockies

Mountain Classics Collection 3

James Outram
Foreword by Chic Scott

Born in 1864 in London, England, James Outram was a Church of England clergyman, mountaineer, author, businessman, militia officer and Orangeman who came to Canada at the turn of the 20th century after travelling and climbing throughout Europe. First published in 1905, *In the Heart of the Canadian Rockies* is Outram's record of his adventures and exploits in the early years of the 20th century among the massive mountains straddling the Alberta–British Columbia boundary.

ISBN 978-1-894765-96-1
$22.95, Softcover

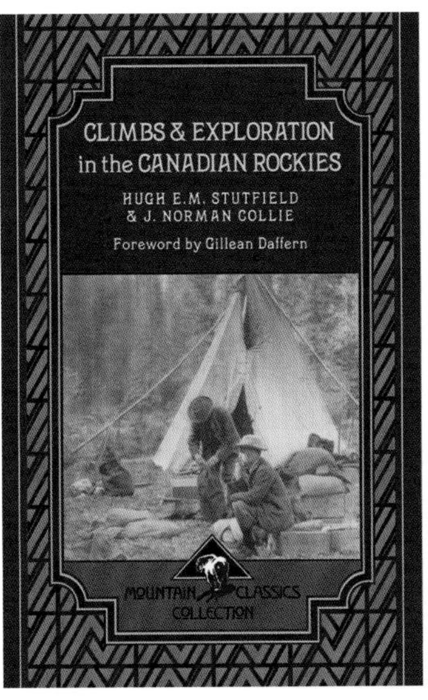

Climbs & Exploration in the Canadian Rockies

Mountain Classics Collection 4

Hugh E.M. Stutfield & J. Norman Collie
Foreword by Gillean Daffern

First published in 1903, *Climbs & Exploration in the Canadian Rockies* details the mountaineering adventures of Hugh Stutfield and J. Norman Collie while the two were together during various explorations in the area north of Lake Louise, Alberta. Between 1898 and 1902, Stutfield and Collie journeyed through the mountain towns, valleys and passes of the Rockies, where Collie completed numerous first ascents and discovered fresh views of Lake Louise and the Columbia Icefield.

ISBN 978-1-897522-06-6

$22.95, Softcover

The Rockies of Canada

Mountain Classics Collection 5

Walter Wilcox
Foreword by Neil Wedin

First published in 1900, *The Rockies of Canada* is based on one of the first major works to be written about the mountains of western Canada, *Camping in the Canadian Rockies* (1896). Focusing on the escapades and first ascents of the "Lake Louise Club," a group of relatively inexperienced climbers from Yale University and elsewhere in the eastern United States, this book offers the reader a glimpse not only of the remarkable beauty and grandeur of Banff, Lake Louise and the Rocky Mountains, but also the danger and rigours these early adventurers experienced nearly every day.

ISBN 978-1-897522-14-1
$19.95, Softcover

On the Roof of the Rockies

Mountain Classics Collection 6

Lewis Ransome Freeman

Foreword by Emerson Sanford & Janice Sanford Beck

This book details the amazing efforts undertaken by Lewis Freeman and Byron Harmon to scientifically explore and comprehensively photograph during their 70-day, 500-mile journey the most stunning regions of the Canadian Rockies and Columbia Mountains. With a guide, a wrangler, a cook, 16 horses, two dogs, some carrier pigeons and hundreds of pounds of what was then state-of-the-art photography, moviemaking and radio equipment, the group journeyed through the area contemplating the routes of earlier explorers, facing violent storms and ultimately preserving historic views of pristine wilderness for future generations.

ISBN 978-1-897522-46-2

Black & White Photos

$19.95, Softcover

No Ordinary Woman

The Story of Mary Schäffer Warren

Janice Sanford Beck

Artist, photographer, writer, world traveller and, above all, explorer, Mary Schäffer Warren overcame the limited expectations of women at the turn of the 19th century in order to follow her dreams.

ISBN 978-0-921102-82-3

Colour and Black & White Photos

$24.95, Softcover

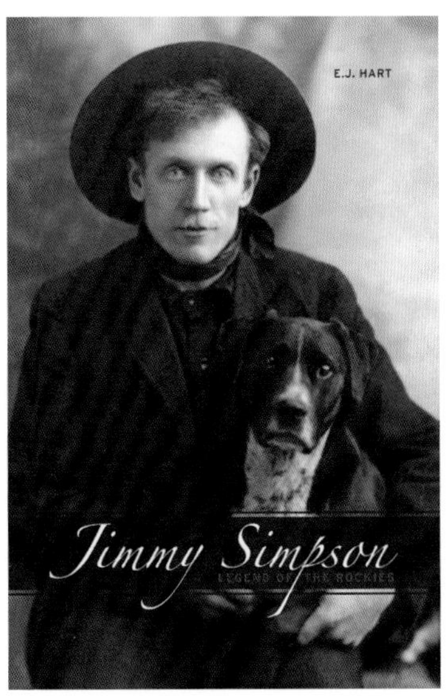

Jimmy Simpson

Legend of the Rockies

E.J. Hart

The Stoney Indians called him "Nashan-esen" meaning "wolverine-go-quick" because of his speed in travelling on snowshoes over the rugged landscape of the Candian Rockies. This book is the story of Jimmy Simpson's 80-year epic as one of the most important guides, outfitters, lodge operators, hunters, naturalists and artists in the Canadian Rockies.

ISBN 978-1-897522-25-7
Black & White Photos
$24.95, Softcover

50 Roadside Panoramas

In the Canadian Rockies

Dave Birrell

Dave Birrell brings you 50 panoramas taken from highway viewpoints in the Canadian Rockies and the Eastern Slopes between Yellowhead Pass and Waterton. Photographs are accompanied by knowledgeable text, providing you with the fascinating stories behind the names of geographical features: mountains, passes, valleys and lakes.

ISBN 978-0921102-65-6

Black & White Photos, Maps

$24.95, Softcover

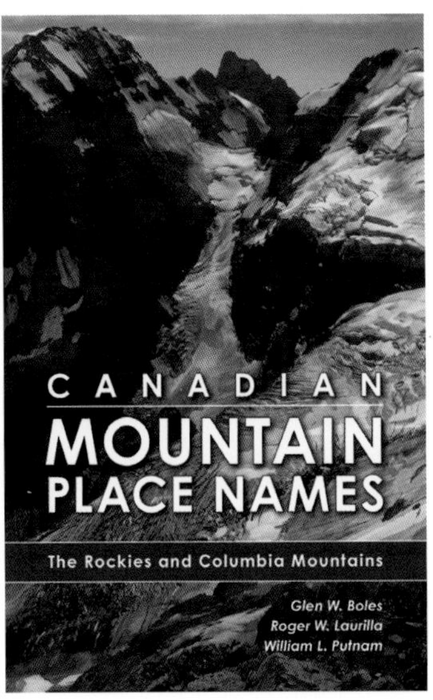

Canadian Mountain Place Names

The Rockies and Columbia Mountains

Glen W. Boles, Roger W. Laurilla, William L. Putnam

This is an entertaining and informative treatise on the toponymy of this increasingly popular alpine region, featuring the names of peaks, rivers, lakes and other geographic landmarks.

ISBN 978-1-894765-79-4
Black & White Photos, Line Drawings
$19.95, Softcover

Pushing the Limits

The Story of Canadian Mountaineering

Chic Scott

Journeying to the summits, the crags and the gyms, from the West Coast to Québec and from the Yukon to the Rockies, Chic introduces his readers to early mountain pioneers and modern-day climbing athletes.

ISBN 978-0921102-59-5

Colour and Black & White Photos, Prints, Maps

$59.95, Hardcover